How to Build a

Second-Income Fortune

in Your Spare Time

Tyler G. Hicks

Parker Publishing Company, Inc. $$$$$$$$$$$$$$$$$$$$$$$$$$$$$$$$ $$$$$$$$$

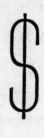

How to Build a

Second-Income Fortune

in Your Spare Time

$$ *West Nyack, N.Y.*

*How to Build a Second-Income Fortune
In Your Spare Time*, by Tyler G. Hicks

© 1965 by Parker Publishing Company, Inc., W. Nyack, N.Y.

Library of Congress Catalog Card Number: 65–11883

Reward Edition . . . . . December, 1973

Fifth Printing . . . . . April, 1978

PRINTED IN THE UNITED STATES OF AMERICA

—B&P

What This Book Will Do for You

You live today in an age of inflated money—a time in which almost every necessity, and luxury, costs you more than it did last year, or last month. To live well in this age you need a larger income.

A bigger paycheck seems, at first, to be the answer. But every time you get a raise you probably find yourself spending all, or almost all, of it on necessities. If you're like many people, you never catch up, you can always use more income.

To solve your money problems today you need a new, powerful, proven, positive approach. This book gives you exactly that—a powerful new key to greater wealth and happiness. This valuable new key to financial success—*a second-income spare-time fortune*—can be the most important discovery of your life.

For this momentous key opens new worlds of freedom to you by providing better vacations, improved education for your children and yourself, opportunities for fuller expression of your personality, more of the possessions you treasure, and—best of all—freedom from nagging money worries that lessen your enjoyment of life.

What do you need to use this new key? Must you be a genius, an empire builder, a millionaire? No. All you need is the desire and courage to follow the step-by-step procedures given in this book. For if you follow these powerful, proven procedures you are almost certain to build a profitable spare-time second-income fortune.

What's more, you can start with little cash—less than $100 in some ventures. And you will continue to receive your regular income while you build one or more sources of spare-time dollars. For this book shows you why you are better off *keeping* your present job while expanding your income with those lucrative, useful, helpful spare-time dollars.

Let's not waste time—let's get started on building your spare-time second-income fortune *now*. Just turn to Chapter 1 to begin what may be the greatest adventure of your life. Join the smart-money people of this world—rocket yourself to a new fortune that will give you the security and possessions you've always wanted.

Good luck!

TYLER G. HICKS

v

Contents

How to Build a

Second-Income Fortune

in Your Spare Time

1

Money *is* important to everyone—to you, to me, to our relatives and friends. The trite clichés of the crowd—money is the root of all evil, it won't buy happiness— are the lame excuses of those who cannot or will not exert themselves enough to earn more money. Even the ancients realized its importance; their quick reply when questioned about the usefulness of money was: "Money answereth all things."

If you believed differently, you wouldn't be reading this book. While you may not believe that money answers all

Money *Is* Important

—to Everyone

things, you do believe money is worth the effort it takes to get it.

Money *is* good—it can lead to many worthwhile acts. Any evil attributed to money springs not from the money itself, but from the people seeking or using the money. And of all the money in circulation today, far more is used for worthwhile purposes than for evil.

In many ways money is a measure of a person's efforts in life. While you know many people who work hard but accumulate little money, you also know others who are building a sizeable second-income spare-time reserve of funds through steady work and careful management.

Money *is* important to everyone—young or old. In this book you will learn how to make your belief in the importance of money pay off. You will acquire sure-fire money-making and money-handling skills. To start you on the road to greater wealth through a second-income fortune, this chapter shows clearly what a spare-time income will do for you. Establishing the advantages of wealth firmly in mind is your first step to greater financial freedom. Let's take that step—a step that may be the most important one of your lifetime—*now*.

KNOW HOW MONEY WILL HELP YOU

There are at least twelve ways in which money earned in your spare time will make your life better. This added income will give you: (1) material possessions, (2) recreation, (3) education, (4) travel, (5) medical care, (6) secure retirement, (7) friends, (8) greater self-confidence, (9) fuller enjoyment of life, (10) freer self-expression, (11) incentives for greater achievement, and (12) a chance to make charitable contributions.

Let's take a quick look at each. Knowing how money will help you will build your drive for a greater income. Spare-time second-income paths to greater wealth will be easier for you to find and follow. As you read about each way in which money will help you, visualize the changes that will occur in *your* life.

BUILD YOUR POSSESSIONS

Everyone wants possessions of some kind—a home, lovely furniture, a new automobile, a boat, and many others. You've met people who say money isn't important. They say they don't want to "clutter" their lives with a home, washing machine, dryer, or other "gadgets." All they want is a sports car, or a ski lodge, hi-fi set, or some similar favorite item. But what is this but a possession? Watch these people and you'll see that within a year or so after acquiring their favorite item they'll be longing for something new and different. Within a short time their lives are as "cluttered" as anyone's.

Possessions can bring you happiness, comfort, relaxation, and enjoyment. A beautiful home, well-tailored clothing, a car of your choice—all these, and many others, can make your life fuller, more meaningful.

Money enables you to acquire the possessions you prize. And the more you strive for the money the greater will be your enjoyment of your possessions.

Take fifteen minutes out of your busy schedule and do three things: (1) Decide what possessions you would most enjoy. (2) Make a list of these and the price of each. (3) Assign a date on which you would like to acquire each possession. Don't assign the same date to each possession—instead, use a schedule that gives you one possession next month; another in three months, and so on.

Save your schedule list and check it off as you acquire each possession. Watching your possessions grow will give you an enormous boost in self-confidence. You will also learn how to predict accurately the time needed to amass a given amount of money. Later chapters show you how to plan for and acquire, by means of a second-income spare-time fortune, the money you need for any purpose.

RECREATION RENEWS YOUR ENERGIES

I'm a boat "nut"—at least that's the way my family describes me. Every weekend of the summer you'll find me cruising in my twin-engine cabin cruiser. This boat renews my energies—it gives me greater strength to follow my busy winter schedule of writing books, teaching, practicing my profession, and holding a full-time executive position.

Does recreation cost money? Certainly it does. Even a simple picnic costs money. But any recreation—golf, swimming, boating, hiking, camping—is worth every dollar you put into it. Look at the wealthy men you know, or those you've read about. All have some favorite recreation—Bing Crosby his boats and golf, the late Herbert Hoover his fishing, Crawford Greenewalt his bird photographs.

Money allows you to pursue the recreation that most interests you.

Certainly much recreation, like walking, is free. But most people seek more than walking; they want to do something that almost always seems to cost money. Recreation you pay for may not be any more healthful than the free kind—but it is often more enjoyable.

Choose your favorite recreation today—let it be skin-diving, chess, or gardening—but choose it. Make a list of what you'll need to begin. Get some books and magazines devoted to your recreation. Read them thoroughly. Determine how much money you'll need to get started. Set a date for starting your new pursuit. Then make plans showing how you'll acquire the money for your equipment. Begin working towards your goal.

SAVE FOR EDUCATION

Your own or your children's education can bring greater joy and appreciation of life than many other investments you make. You deserve a good education, no matter what your age. This can be formal education in a college or school of your choice. Or it can be a correspondence course, regular reading of good books, listening to foreign-language records, special instruction in tennis or swimming, or any other skill you may wish to acquire.

Your children deserve the best education you can afford for them. Cutting corners on a child's education is foolish economy. What's more, you'll regret your penny-pinching attitude when your child is grown and struggling to earn a good income.

Education costs money. A year at a better college or university can cost $3,500 or more. With more than one child to educate you can look forward to total college costs of $25,000 or more.

Where will you acquire this sum? Certainly not from a $150-per-week job, even if your wife works. Even with a $250-per-week job you will find it difficult to save money for your children's education. Why? Because almost everyone today has the habit of allowing his standard of living to creep ahead of his income. Result: most of us must borrow to pay for the big items such as a college education, an automobile, or a trip to Europe.

Face up to the future educational costs you must meet for your children and yourself. Draw a picture of your income and expenses for the years during which you'll have large educational costs. If this period is several years off, start with your present salary, as John W., an airline executive, did in Figure 1. Try to predict the amount of each raise you may receive, and the date on which it will be granted, just as John did. Then draw the earnings line.

If your sketch shows your educational expenses will outrun your regular income, take immediate action to earn the money you'll need. How? Build a spare-time second income. See the later chapters in this book for hundreds of sure-fire second-income suggestions. Even if you don't earn all the money you need, the income you do receive will be a big help to your budget. However, our aim is to help you earn *all* the money you need—and then some!

TRAVEL BROADENS YOUR HORIZONS

"Travel teaches toleration," wrote Disraeli. It also teaches many other important lessons. For you too will find, as did Mme. de Stael, the French novelist, that "the more I see of other countries the more I love my own."

Travel costs money, whether you go by low-cost bicycle or the latest jet airliner. And if you have a family, your expenses will be more than just transportation and lodging. You'll also have to pay for the care of your children while you're gone (unless you have a well-fixed mother or mother-in-law), or take the children with you. Either way, costs will be higher.

You can pay for travel in two ways: save and then go; or go and then pay—on time. But no matter which way you pay, you must earn the money.

Earning the money to travel can be easier if you set goals. To do this first choose the vacation trip you'd like to take and get full information on transportation and accommodations costs from your travel agent. Choose a date for the trip. Next you must decide how you'll earn the money for your trip and take immediate steps to earn the amount you need, plus an extra $1,000. Use the remaining chapters of this book as a guide to earning this money, in your spare time. For as Ralph Waldo Emerson observed, "The world is his, who has money to go over it."

ADD ZEST TO LIFE WITH PROPER MEDICAL CARE

Medical and dental care expenses are probably the most difficult to

Figure 1—Typical Expense-Planning Chart

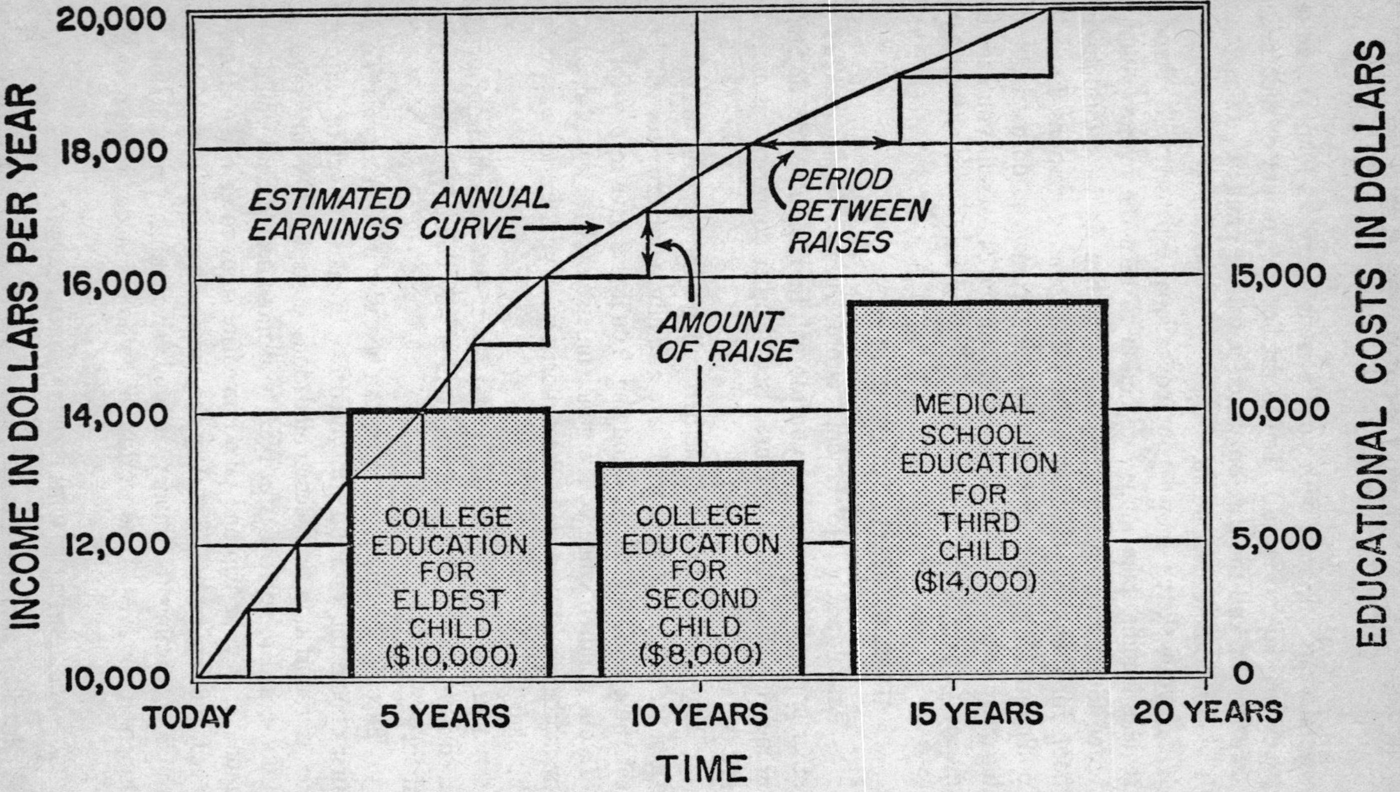

EDUCATIONAL COSTS IN DOLLARS

15,000

10,000

5,000

0

INCOME IN DOLLARS PER YEAR

20,000

18,000

16,000

14,000

12,000

10,000

TODAY

5 YEARS

10 YEARS

15 YEARS

20 YEARS

TIME

ESTIMATED ANNUAL EARNINGS CURVE

PERIOD BETWEEN RAISES

AMOUNT OF RAISE

COLLEGE EDUCATION FOR ELDEST CHILD ($10,000)

COLLEGE EDUCATION FOR SECOND CHILD ($8,000)

MEDICAL SCHOOL EDUCATION FOR THIRD CHILD ($14,000)

predict because you never know when they will occur. Also, the costs of both types of care are rising; hospitalization and medical insurance seldom completely cover all major costs.

Proper medical and dental care are the most important investments you'll ever make. What is anything in life worth if you have a sick, diseased body? Money, position, reputation and friends are of little use unless you are healthy. No material possession is worth acquiring if, in doing so, you damage your health.

James K., a publishing executive, had very poor teeth. Over the years he delayed going to the dentist as long as possible. When he did visit the dentist, he had the minimum amount of work done because he thought "every dentist is out to overcharge me." One day, while looking in the mirror he was shocked to notice that his teeth were yellowed and discolored. Several gaps, where missing teeth had never been replaced, looked like black holes in his mouth. Later that day he mentioned this experience to his secretary. "Yes," she said, "you don't smile too often because subconsciously you realize that your teeth are unattractive."

James K. made an immediate appointment with a dentist. He resolved he would have his "entire mouth fixed." And he did, even though the cost was $1,643. To have this job done, James K. had to work a little harder and cut back on his country club activities. Today he says, "I never realized how gratifying it could be to spend money on my body. With my teeth in good condition I smile more often. I feel better when talking to my superiors at work. Every morning and evening when I look in the mirror I say to myself, 'That was the best money I ever spent.'"

Do you need some medical or dental work? Sit down immediately and decide how you will pay for it. Next, choose a way to earn the money in your spare time. Don't delay; have the medical or dental work done. The same goes for any medical or dental attention needed by members of your family. One of the greatest advantages of having money is the freedom it gives you to obtain the proper medical and dental care. For when you feel well everything in life seems, and is, much more worthwhile.

RETIREMENT SHOULDN'T BE A NIGHTMARE

Yet it is for some people. Most often the biggest cause of trouble for these older people is inadequate income. Another cause of difficulty is lack of interest in worthwhile activities.

Build a bigger income today so that you can enjoy part of it now and part of it when you retire. Develop a spare-time business now; enjoy current income from it. Continue this business into your retirement and the interest and zest it adds to your mind can help prolong your life.

Being able to look forward to a secure retirement will give you greater peace of mind while you are working. Once you retire from your current activities you will have more time to pursue your special interests. If you can combine your hobbies, a spare-time business, and an adequate income, you should have a long and rewarding retirement.

Begin now to plan for your retirement. If your present position doesn't offer a pension, investigate ways in which you can set up your own pension fund. Determine the cost and resolve to earn the needed money. If a spare-time business will furnish the cash needed, read the later chapters in this book for hundreds of hints on how to earn extra money.

MONEY BRINGS FRIENDS

"But they aren't true friends," you say. This is debatable. Having money to travel, to pursue your favorite recreation, and to live where you wish, opens new possibilities for friendship. The people you meet under circumstances of your own choosing can be just as true friends as those met under any other conditions. What's more, when you have the greater freedom of action that money offers, you can exert more care in your choice of friends.

Loneliness besets many people, particularly in their later years. With money available these older people can take part in activities that will bring them in closer contact with people of their own age. Younger people tend to have fewer problems with loneliness. But even for them, the opportunities for the varied activities that money affords, can lead to more desirable friends. Attractive social contacts can be shared and enjoyed by everyone in your family. What's more, money permits you a wider circle of friends. For example, you can have friends at a country club, yacht club, fraternal group, bowling association, religious group or political party. All these and similar activities require that you spend money, even if only indirectly for transportation, a baby sitter, or special clothing.

Since childhood you've probably been told that "money won't buy friends." To a certain extent this is true. But money can put you in places where interesting people go. So rid yourself of your old thinking patterns by recognizing this fact. Get out and earn the extra money you need to go to these places. Then go and make some new friends. It's really easy when you have the money. For even the Bible says, "Wealth maketh many friends."

MONEY AND SELF-CONFIDENCE GO TOGETHER

There's nothing quite so reassuring as having money in your pocket. Or money in the bank and blue-chip stocks in a safe deposit box. Regardless of what critics of the wealthy may say, money *does* bring self-confidence to those who earned it honestly. Just think—all you need are a few paper greenbacks in your wallet, or a slim checkbook backed by what the banker calls "good" deposits, and you can go anywhere, buy anything available for money.

Many people who have given up the pursuit of money because they've tried and failed, undervalue the importance of money to a person's self-assurance. Yet the practical facts of life show that most people's self-confidence increases as they acquire more money. Somerset Maugham, always a wise observer of people, said, "Money is like a sixth sense without which you cannot make a complete use of the other five." Long before Mr. Maugham was born, William Somerville, another Englishman, wrote: "Let all the learned say what they can; It's ready money that makes the man."

Money dissolves many feelings of inadequacy; it alleviates what Maugham called the degrading "constant anxiety about one's means of livelihood." So disregard those who tell you money means nothing where self-confidence is concerned. These people, as George Bernard Shaw wrote, ". . . are always blaming their circumstances for what they are. I don't believe in circumstances. The people who get on in this world are the people who get up and look for the circumstances they want, and, if they can't find them, make them." Remember—money makes the man.

If you've ever known that wonderful feeling of renewed self-confidence because you had extra dollars in your pocket—get out and earn some more. This book shows you how to build a second-income fortune in your spare time.

USE MONEY TO ENJOY LIFE MORE

"It is better to live rich than die rich," wrote Samuel Johnson. That worthy gentleman appreciated money—not for itself alone, but rather for the things and experiences only money can buy; the fulfillment of the desires that can help you live and enjoy life to the fullest.

Some people derive their greatest pleasures from strolling in a public park and observing the pedestrians, plants, and scenery. Others require Cadillacs, yachts, hunting lodges, or trips around the world. Each man makes his choice and lives by it.

What gives you the greatest enjoyment in life? Do you know? If you do not, sit down some evening in a quiet room and review your interests and desires. Is skiing an irresistible attraction? Or do you prefer trips to foreign lands? Chances are that your greatest joys in life will come from activities costing money.

Pleasures that cost money can be just as rewarding as those that are free. "The best things in life are free" is not true when applied to an adult world. All pleasures cost something—whether that cost is measured in dollars, time, energy, or other intangibles.

A substantial bank balance enables you to do interesting things, permits you to help those less fortunate than yourself, brings joy to your family. So use the money you have to get more out of life. You have but one life on this earth. Enjoy it now, doing the things that bring you genuine pleasure.

MONEY MAKES SELF-EXPRESSION EASIER

With money in your pocket or in the bank you can be more relaxed. You have fewer worries about what people think of you. If they don't like you—fine. You can find other friends, and so can they.

A man or woman who is constantly pinched for money becomes fearful of the people who control his income. If a man has a family he worries about being fired from his job. When he spends a few dollars on his hobby he feels guilty because he is depriving his family of things they would otherwise have. The constant pressure produced by the lack of money prevents him from acting the way he wishes. His self-expression is cramped; he feels trapped.

Acting the way you wish to is a wonderful freedom. As long as you don't abuse this freedom, you will relish the money-made independence that permits you to express yourself as you wish. You will lead a fuller life, free of stifling worry over where your next few hundred dollars are coming from. Being able to do as you please enables you to achieve more worthwhile goals in life. For, when a man acts the way he believes he should, he often achieves more than when he is forced into a pattern by others who control his income.

If you desire freedom of self-expression, use this as an incentive to earn more money. Added to the other incentives mentioned earlier in this chapter, the desire for self-expression can be a powerful stimulus to your money-earning drive. Emerson wrote that "Money, which represents the prose of life, is, in its effects and laws, as beautiful as roses."

WEALTH BUILDERS ACHIEVE MORE

Many people who are not motivated by the drive for money, or who have failed in their efforts, criticize money-seekers as selfish. Yet as long ago as 42 B.C., Publilius Syrus wrote, "Money alone sets all the world in motion."

The wealth builders of today, be their fortunes large or small, are the doers in this world. Men and women who build wealth for themselves and their families are people of action. They get things done. Seeking wealth is not selfish. Why shouldn't you and your family have the best in life? There is nothing wrong with seeking and acquiring money, provided your means are honest. And the only means we recommend in this book are completely honest.

So, disregard the complainers and the frustrated—seek what you desire. Always remember that in building wealth, you are helping others besides yourself. Never be ashamed of earning money—or spending it. In earning money you are rendering a valuable service to someone; if your work wasn't worth several times what you are paid, your income would cease. In spending money you are giving someone work. And someone else profits from this work. So the careful earning and spending of money helps build a better economy for everyone.

Keep one thought in mind at all times: *Wealth builders are important.* They are more important than all the complainers and frustrated put together. For, as Rousseau wrote, "Money is the seed of money, and the first guinea is sometimes more difficult to acquire than the second million."

CHARITY BRINGS JOY

The wealthiest men the world has known—John D. Rockefeller, Andrew Carnegie, J. Paul Getty, Alfred P. Sloan, and many others—derived much satisfaction from helping needy causes and people. While *giving* money away may seem foolish after you've worked so hard to acquire it, real joy awaits you when you contribute to a worthwhile cause.

You can learn some of the joy of giving by volunteering your time and energy to a good cause. For instance, before I could afford to contribute money to worthwhile groups, my wife and I often took one or more orphan boys into our home for a weekend, even though we had three children of our own. The joy of watching these boys at a family dinner table, sleeping in a room of their own, romping in a backyard pool, and steering a big powerboat, more than repaid any slight expense or bother entailed in their visit. Today we contribute money to orphan homes and derive much satisfaction—almost as much as when we had the boys in our home.

Giving money to needy causes and people makes you feel good inside. The act of giving seems to blot out many of the incidents in your life about which you feel some guilt. While such "buying" of peace of mind may be criticized by some people, the practical result of generous giving may be a release of tension. When this reduction of tension is combined with the warmth generated by giving and the beneficial results of the gift, everyone can truly say that charity brings joy.

You will never regret donating money for good causes. And there are thousands of worthwhile uses you can find for money. A good friend of mine, a top-notch electronics engineer, had some spare cash that he wanted to put to work helping someone. One day he heard of a young man whose greatest ambition in life was to attend engineering school. But the boy lacked funds and had little chance of earning enough to pay for his education. The electronics engineer offered to lend the boy the money, free of interest, to be paid back over a period of years after graduation. The boy jumped at the offer, graduated with honors, and recently made his final payment on the loan. He will never forget the favor the electronics engineer did for him; if that young man can ever afford to help someone in a similar manner, I assure you he will.

Using your money is only half the fun of having it—the other half is earning it. Learn how to earn more so that you can give more. This book will show you how to pyramid your present income into a spare-time fortune.

MONEY IS GOOD, POWERFUL, WORTHWHILE

Money *is* important to everyone—to you, to me, to our children, our relatives, our friends. Money is good, powerful and worthwhile. Every honest effort you make to earn money brings rewards in one way or another. If you are successful and earn the money you seek, fine. Even if you fail, you gain experience. This experience will help you make your *next* effort more successful.

The book you are now reading shows you exactly how to prevent false starts in building your spare-time second-income fortune. It gives you hundreds of tested, proven, valuable steps to greater wealth through a spare-time income. In this chapter you explored a few of the benefits of having money. There are many others you can add to those listed. Only *you* can decide if you want those benefits. I'm sure you do.

So turn to Chapter 2 and take the next powerful and confident step towards greater wealth through a spare-time income.

Your next step towards greater spare-time wealth is to answer, as honestly and objectively as you can, one simple question: AM I A NATURAL WEALTH BUILDER?

Think of the wealthy people you know or have read about. Many of them seem to have a knack for making large sums of money. Often their knowledge of the technical aspects of their work will be limited. Yet, when it comes to their business knowledge—to the skills needed to earn big money quickly—these people are tops. Of course, many top money makers

| 2 |

Test Your Wealth-
Building Potential

are also first-rate craftsmen—like Frank I. Fletcher, the highest paid ad-writer of all time. Starting his career as an $18-a-week stenographer, Fletcher wound up receiving $1,000 for each short advertisement he wrote. He freelanced for 47 years at this rate of pay, and was long reputed to be the world's highest paid advertising writer.

Many natural wealth builders, like Fletcher and others, have eight or more important characteristics. Here are these characteristics. See how many *you* possess today.

The natural wealth builder is seldom a loner—instead he usually relies on directing the efforts of others to bring him a profit. Andrew Carnegie realized this when he said, "It marks a big step in a man's development when he comes to realize that other men can be called in to help him do a better job than he can do alone." Carnegie built a fortune using this principle.

The natural wealth builder is decisive—he makes decisions quickly. And, usually, these decisions are correct. Harry Lefrak built an apart-ment-house empire on a quick decision. Arriving in New York as a 20-year-old immigrant with only $4.00 in his pocket, he started his career by shoveling snow. Seeing no future in this, he quickly shifted to the build-ing industry. This decision ultimately led to the construction of a $150-million, 40-acre building complex housing 25,000 people—Lefrak Village. This is only one example of how a natural wealth builder parlayed a quick, accurate decision into a personal fortune.

Natural wealth builders are pushers—they go after what they want with gusto, and don't stop until they achieve their objective. Harry J. Grant, outstanding editor of the *Milwaukee Journal*, quit high school at the age of 15 after his freshman year to earn money to support his widowed mother. At 35 he retired to England, after making a fortune in the textile business. Later, he returned to the United States and quickly became president and editor of the *Milwaukee Journal*. He built this newspaper to the point where, for several years, it carried more advertis-ing than any publication in the world. Eventually he turned the ownership of the paper over to its employees. He not only planned the ownership transfer, he also provided his employees with the money to purchase the paper. Grant used his natural drive to build a fortune that benefitted thou-sands of people.

Quick analytical ability is a trait most spare-time natural wealth builders turn into profit. The natural wealth builder is never afraid or too lazy to think. In fact, he always seems to be thinking. His mind continually reaches out for new ideas, new ways to build wealth. He enjoys figuring the chances for the success of a new venture, the percentage of profit he can make on a deal. The constant preoccupation with numbers gives him the ready ability to analyze a situation quickly and accurately.

Men and women born to build wealth are constantly alert. They listen intently when people talk; they observe people, businesses, neighborhoods. This constant alertness serves to satisfy, in part, their hunger for new knowledge about business, money, and profit opportunities. The natural wealth builder never lulls himself into inaction by sticking to a job that is nothing more than a security-lined rut. Instead, he searches for new ways to earn a spare-time second-income dollar, new means for producing a profit. He finds that profit-seeking is an irresistible challenge. For, like the famous economist Lord Keynes, natural wealth builders believe that "the engine which drives enterprise is not thrift, but profit."

The natural wealth builder is persistent—he keeps after his objective until he achieves it. Three women—Marian Knobler, Magda Bierman, and Dorothy Arden—built a women's wear manufacturing firm from scratch, starting with only $2,000. Nine years later the firm had annual sales of over $2.5 million. When asked what made them succeed, the first trait they mentioned was perseverance. Persistent pursuit of a financial goal is almost certain to bring favorable results. The natural wealth builder recognizes this fact and keeps after his objective. He pursues his goal even though his "smarter" friends say he's wasting his time.

Wealth builders are born risk-takers. They are not afraid to risk their savings on a business proposition they think has promise. Most wealth builders are willing to save money to invest at a later date. But while they are building a spare-time fortune they dislike saving money simply to be thrifty. They want to put their money to work because they believe that money is the seed of money. The "smart-money" wealth builders, who are accustomed to making profits of 33 per cent or more per year on their money, are not satisfied with three or four per cent bank interest. That's why they're willing to take risks.

Borrowing money to make money is popular with natural wealth builders. They dislike borrowing money simply to spend it—they'd rather borrow money to invest. The natural wealth builder has his fun spending the profits.

TEST YOUR WEALTH-BUILDING TRAITS

Here's a handy checklist to help you determine if you have natural wealth-building traits. Take this test now. The results will show you the best course towards building your own spare-time second-income fortune in the shortest time.

ARE YOU A NATURAL WEALTH BUILDER?

1. Do you ever stop to compute the seller's profit on something you buy? ___ Yes ___ No
2. Have you regularly tried to determine the dealer's cost of large items you buy (auto, home, boat, etc.)? ___ Yes ___ No
3. Did you ever borrow money to invest in a profit-making project? ___ Yes ___ No
4. Do you own any common stocks? ___ Yes ___ No
5. If you had money to invest in the stock market would you choose common stocks instead of a mutual fund? ___ Yes ___ No
6. Do you try to be creative about earning money by seeking new ways to produce income? ___ Yes ___ No
7. Have you ever set yourself a specific financial goal to achieve—like $5,000 or $10,000? ___ Yes ___ No
8. Can you work congenially with others for extended periods of time? ___ Yes ___ No
9. Do you make decisions quickly? ___ Yes ___ No
10. Do you usually finish what you start (a job around the house, a book, a course)? ___ Yes ___ No
11. Can you analyze a situation or problem quickly? ___ Yes ___ No
12. Do you watch the newspapers and magazines you read for helpful money-making ideas? ___ Yes ___ No
13. Are you persistent in your pursuit of the things in life that interest you? ___ Yes ___ No
14. Does taking a risk with money frighten you? ___ Yes ___ No

ARE YOU A NATURAL WEALTH BUILDER? (*cont.*)

15. Would you rather take a chance in a business of your own than work for a fixed salary?   ____ Yes ____ No

Score your wealth-building chances according to the number of *yes* answers you checked: 15—excellent; this book will be a good review of ideas you may have overlooked; 10 to 14—you can hit the big money if you really try, but you need this book to help you; 5 to 9—you need this book and its ideas to guide you to wealth; 0 to 5—study every word of this book if you want to earn more money in your spare time.

NATURAL WEALTH BUILDERS ARE RARE

There are few natural wealth builders. The man who naturally amasses a large fortune during his lifetime, starting with little capital, is rare. Certainly, hundreds of new millionaires have made their fortunes since 1950. But did you ever think of the millions of other people who didn't become millionaires during that time? Many of these people could have amassed sizeable fortunes if they knew how.

Some people *learn* the secrets of the natural wealth builder. They *train* themselves to use the same techniques as the natural wealth builder. The *trained wealth builder*, as we will call him, can also build a spare-time fortune. But the size of his fortune will depend on how well he has trained himself and how effectively he duplicates the methods of the natural wealth builder. Just as a trained athlete can out-perform the untrained amateur, the "natural" athlete can out-perform the trained athlete who has little natural ability. Thus the natural wealth builder may amass a larger fortune than the trained wealth builder—but the trained man will amass much more money than the untrained person who hungers for wealth but does not know how to acquire it.

WEALTH TRAINING HELPS EVERYONE

Suppose you scored low on the test earlier in this chapter. Should you give up seeking a spare-time fortune? No—never. Why? Because most of the modest and medium-sized fortunes amassed in the world today were accumulated by men and women who *learned* the methods of the natural wealth builder. Certainly, a small fortune—say $100,000 to $500,000

—is much more desirable than working for the rest of your life at $6,000 per year.

Wealth-building training, such as this book gives you, *can* help you. It can make the difference between a routine life and a full, rich life. Even if the training adds only $50,000 to your lifetime income, you will have benefitted many times over from your investment of time and money in this book.

To derive maximum benefit from this wealth-building training you must follow a few simple rules. Study the rules on the following pages and when you know them, go on to Chapter 3. These rules, combined with the thousands of hints and techniques given in the remainder of this book, will put you on the road to an important spare-time second-income fortune. Then you, too, can number yourself among the "smart-money" people of this world

TEN RULES TO DEVELOP WEALTH POWER

1. *Learn to work with people.* You have little chance of building a real second-income fortune without the help of other people. A few loners—usually inventors and authors—make big money without the help of others. But the biggest spare-time fortunes are made when a man or woman with ideas joins forces with talented people having many skills. For example, Willis H. Carrier, who designed the first practical air-conditioning system, founded Carrier Corporation with the help of six engineers. Carrier was president and chairman of the firm for 33 years, during which time he had help from many of the six engineers with whom he founded the firm.

So, learn to work with people; you can't expect to be an expert in everything. If your field is electronics you'll probably need the help of accountants, lawyers, salesmen, and production managers if you go into business in your spare time. Learn to forget petty rivalries and get to like everyone. Then, do as the natural wealth builder does—when he needs help of any kind, he calls on a friend. *Remember—the friend you make today may help you make your fortune tomorrow.* Knowing how to work with people can be one of the most important tools in your wealth-building kit.

2. *Be decisive—learn how to size up situations quickly.* You can't

earn substantial spare-time money if you take forever to make up your mind. "He who hesitates is lost" is true in most business situations where a large number of people are competing for the same objective.

How do you learn to size up situations quickly? You use all your senses. You look, you feel, you listen; you smell and taste, if necessary. When you encounter a potentially profitable situation, forget everything else, including caution, and concentrate on the facts. Try to absorb as many pertinent facts as quickly as you can. Once you have all the facts in mind, apply your analytical judgment and cautious outlook.

Go over each fact, make a list of pros and cons if you can't evaluate the facts in your mind. If you find one pro equal to one con, cross out each. Should two pros equal, in your judgment, three cons, cross out the five items. After a fast study like this with a pro-and-con balance sheet, you will quickly see which aspect of the situation is strongest because it will have the most factors remaining. Some people perform this type of evaluation mentally and make what appears to be a snap judgment. Actually, they mentally set up a pro-and-con balance sheet and quickly evaluate each of the factors in it. Page 36 shows a pro-and-con balance sheet prepared by a young executive who was wondering if he should try to earn more money by going into a spare-time business. What do you think his decision was?

Try to speed every decision you make. Don't worry about mistakes. If you've been a slow decision-maker in the past you know that slow decisions can be just as wrong as fast ones. The main advantage of the fast decision is that it often permits you to take advantage of a situation before someone else does.

3. *Learn persistence—it pays off.* If you've been a quitter all your life, start changing now. Often the difference between making a spare-time fortune and going broke is a few more hours, days, or weeks of work. Why give up when there's still a chance to succeed? Quitting early can lead you to one failure after another. You get so discouraged that you give up completely and the fortune that might have been, never is.

Do big money-makers give up easily? No; they pursue their objective until they achieve it. For example, Dr. Edward H. Land, inventor of the Land Polaroid camera, tried over three million chemical formulations before he was satisfied with the pictures produced. Ernest Hemingway, one of the world's great writers, often worked for hours to perfect one paragraph.

Persistence can make up for many other deficiencies a person may have. Look around you today. Note that the people who have the most money often are not the most intelligent, the most learned, or the most artistic. Instead, the successful person is often a persistent plodder—a man who knows what he wants and goes after it. His "intelligent" friends may even describe him as so stupid that he doesn't know when to give up. Yet he often winds up with a spare-time fortune far exceeding that of all his "smart" friends.

Begin today to finish what you start. Don't start anything unless you are reasonably sure you will finish it. Begin reinforcing your persistence by finishing simple things, like the reading of this book. Then go on to more difficult tasks, completing each one. Every time you finish a task your confidence will grow. When you begin your search for wealth you will have more confidence and your chances for success will be much greater.

4. *Be constantly alert for new wealth ideas.* Wealth *won't* seek you out—you must seek after it. Begin today to apply this wealth-building rule. Resolve to make every task you perform a step toward building spare-time wealth. Read your newspaper with an eye for second-income wealth opportunities. Study the financial pages for clues to developments that may lead you to wealth. Read the obituaries of wealthy men; you will often find helpful hints in the stories of the successes of these men. Do your daily job with gusto and with the firm intention of turning out the best work possible.

Keep a notebook handy at all times. Jot down each new spare-time wealth idea you find. Don't try to classify the idea when you first find it. Just enter it on a dated page in your notebook. Continue your notebook entries throughout the year, no matter where you are or how you come across an idea. Be alert for new second-income wealth ideas during all your reading, conversations, business meetings and other contacts. For once you *resolve* to find new wealth ideas, your mind will be more eager for them. It will be easier for you to trap and make a note of every good second-income idea you encounter.

Evaluate your notebook ideas at your convenience. Pick a quiet spot and review each page of your notebook. When doing this you may find that the ideas you collected are not directly useful to you. However, by combining two or more ideas you may be able to develop a valuable spare-time money-making scheme.

Begin your campaign of wealth-alertness today. Back up your alertness with a good notebook. The combination can lead you to new money that will help build your fortune.

5. *Recognize the rewards of risk-taking.* There is no safe way to build wealth. Recognize this fact today and your road to a second-income fortune will be much easier. You *must* take risks, if you expect to build wealth. If taking risks scares you, makes you jittery or unhappy, you will have to change your outlook. One way to do this is to take some extra money you have—even as little as $100—and invest it in a risky but promising venture. Mentally write off the money before you invest it. This will reduce some of your fear. Should the venture be successful you will be ready to invest more next time, with less apprehension.

The more risks you take to build spare-time wealth, the greater your chances of hitting it big. This doesn't mean, however, that you should take all your savings and invest them in risky enterprises. Look, instead, for the speculative—but promising—venture. Then invest a portion of your funds in it. The exact amount will depend upon your circumstances. But invest enough so you feel that you are really taking a chance. That way, your return will be somewhat larger, if the second-income project pays off. Risk-taking is an integral part of building wealth—recognize this fact today and you'll be way ahead of others who hunger for wealth the "safe" way.

6. *Never be ashamed to borrow money to make money.* Some of the largest spare-time fortunes are built on borrowed money. The natural wealth builder understands and uses credit to the fullest. He buys real estate with a minimum investment of his capital. As a stock market speculator he uses margin whenever he can. Certainly, borrowing money costs money. But if you can make money using other people's capital, you can expand your profit potential far beyond that offered by your own resources.

People (banks, mortgage specialists, loan firms, and many government agencies) are in business to lend money. They *want* you to borrow, if you have a good credit standing and you intend to use the money for worthwhile purposes. Understand this fact of life and you'll have fewer problems when you apply for a loan. Also, you'll soon see that to borrow money to earn money is one of the smartest moves you can make as a spare-time fortune builder.

7. *Be time-conscious at all times.* "Time is money" is the famous remark of Ben Franklin. Time-consciousness is directly related to spare-time wealth building. There has seldom been a man who built his second-income fortune without first recognizing the importance of time in his financial plans.

Just think of a few results of being time-conscious. You (a) evaluate your efforts in terms of their financial return to you, (b) see each day as a block of time to be devoted to building your spare-time fortune, (c) size up people, and the time you spend with them, in terms of your financial objectives, and (d) set up time goals for achieving your second-income wealth aims.

Become time-conscious today. When beginning a new venture you'll often find that, as one spare-time fortune builder said, ". . . practically your whole life is going to be devoted to its success." In the early days of a new second-income venture you may work for as little as 50 cents per hour. Later on, when the venture is successful, you may refuse to work for anything less than $50 per hour. In the early efforts to establish the venture, your time-consciousness will tell you that the low hourly rate is worthwhile because you are establishing an equity. At a later date, with business booming, you may feel that your health and golf game are more important than a spare-time income of $50 or more an hour. So don't delay—resolve now to become time-conscious; for delay, as Alex Lewyt so wisely observed, ". . . is responsible for more failures, more lack of success than any other circumstance." His outstandingly successful vacuum cleaner shows the results of avoiding delays.

8. *Be a finisher—finish what you start.* Don't give up; you almost always lose when you abandon your efforts before you finish the task you set out to perform. Spare-time wealth won't run, walk, or crawl to you— you must go after it. If you quit when halfway to your goal the money you seek will stay where it is and your pockets will be empty. "Great works are performed not by strength but by *perseverance*," said Samuel Johnson, who knew the secrets of accomplishing great works.

Begin by finishing every small task you start. Go on to larger undertakings, like preparing *complete* plans for your financial future. Don't give up in the middle of your planning; complete the plans even though you must strain your thinking to do so. Remember—nothing worthwhile is easy. Once you form the habit of finishing your tasks you will gain more self-confidence than you ever thought possible.

9. *Develop your creative powers.* Spare-time wealth comes to the man who can develop new ideas into products or services needed by others. Good ideas *can* be yours, if you develop your creative powers.

Recognize that you *can* become more creative by using these basic guides to develop creative thinking. First, clearly define what you wish to achieve—for example, a certain sum of money, a home in a given area, or a boat of a certain size. Then, list every possible way you might achieve your objective; don't be afraid if some of the methods seem far-fetched or even silly. When ideas stop coming, forget the problem. Do something completely different—go fishing, tramp through the woods, bowl, swim, read. After this, wait—and be alert for the sudden flash of understanding that solves the problem for you; make an immediate note of the solution. Evaluate your idea at a later time, but be sure to put the idea into action as soon as possible.

10. *Visualize, once every day, what money can do for you and your family.* Try to *see* yourself with the money. Imagine the happiness you and your family will derive from the money you seek. See, in your mind's eye, the bank books, stock certificates, real estate, and other possessions the money will bring you. *Feel* the money in your hands. Make it real—and you will acquire what you want.

Don't play down the importance of visualizing the effects of wealth in your life. Every man and woman who has accumulated a fortune had a "money dream" that motivated him. This "money dream" kept him or her alert, ready to trap a new idea, method, or process that could be turned into wealth. Begin now to visualize, daily, *your* money dream.

POINTERS FOR BUILDING YOUR SPARE-TIME WEALTH

Few people are natural wealth builders. Most of us must *learn* how to build wealth for ourselves. You, too, can learn how to build a second-income fortune for yourself. To begin, study the hints in this chapter and put one new pointer into effect in your life each day for the next two weeks. Watch the effect on your search for spare-time wealth. And while you're putting these pointers into action, continue reading this book. It will guide you, step by step, to greater wealth through a spare-time second-income fortune. Then, someday, you, too, may have a large enough fortune to do the things that truly interest and satisfy you.

Talk to the average salaried man or woman about his or her wealth goals and you'll be startled. The *average* man has no idea of his wealth wants or needs. He vaguely desires more money. How much more? He really doesn't know and would have difficulty determining how much he actually needs. Why? Because he never took time to establish his money goals.

Without a wealth goal, you are lost. You flounder from one paycheck to the next. When you receive your paycheck you feel temporarily wealthy. Then you

3

Choose Your

Wealth Goals Today

pay your bills and you're broke—again. This goes on for years. Instead of making headway, your bills mount with your income. You look forward to the day when you "can put a little aside." But that day never arrives. The only time some people's bills are paid off is when their relatives collect the life insurance. Certainly you don't want this to happen to you.

To build a spare-time second-income fortune you need clear, achievable goals. You must *want* to earn money to achieve these goals. You will be successful when people can say about you what the famous Finley Dunne said about a friend of his: "He made money because he honestly loved it."

When you love money you make money one of your lifetime goals. With a clear goal in view, it is easier for you to earn and accumulate money. Let's see how you can put wealth goals to work in earning your spare-time second-income fortune.

HOW WEALTH GOALS HELP YOU

Wealth goals help you in at least four ways. Goals guide your money-making efforts, direct your creative talents towards money-making ideas, set minimum and maximum limits for the amounts you seek, and give you checkpoints for evaluating your progress towards your goals.

As you saw in Chapter 2, the natural wealth builder senses the need for goals. He defines his goals early in his money-seeking efforts and pursues his objectives until he achieves them. Goals are an innate part of his money drive. He sees, as Sallust did nearly two thousand years ago, that "Every man is the architect of his own fortunes."

The trained wealth builder, however, often overlooks the worth of goals during his first attempts to accumulate a spare-time second-income fortune. Yet he desperately needs goals if he is to build a sizeable fortune. Wealth goals help the trained wealth builder develop an innate money drive.

Everyone's financial future is a mystery. While wealth goals do not solve this mystery, they do give you a greater degree of control over your financial future. Often it is this small amount of control that means the difference between outstanding success and a mediocre life. You are now ready to choose your financial goals so that you can begin to build a secure future for yourself and your loved ones.

HOW TO CHOOSE YOUR WEALTH GOALS

There are five important steps in choosing your spare-time wealth goals. None are difficult, but if you don't take each step your chances of success are very slim. Study each step carefully, for as one highly successful fortune-builder said: "Every step on the road to a fortune is important. The man who succeeds knows that there are no shortcuts—so he takes every step carefully."

STEP 1: DECIDE WHAT WEALTH MEANS TO YOU

Wealth and fortune mean different things to people. Some people seek a guaranteed weekly, monthly, or annual income. Thus, one successful Los Angeles spare-time real estate operator set a goal of $2,000 per month rental income from his property. This was his definition of wealth. He concentrated on developing his property until it generated this much spare-time income. His chosen wealth goal had led him to an income level he thought satisfactory. He then had the choice of sitting back and managing his property or developing it further. (Like most ambitious spare-time wealth builders, he did not sit back and relax, but went on to build a larger second-income fortune.)

Some people choose a specific sum of money—say $200,000—as their wealth goal. Disregarding taxes for now (they are discussed later in the book) these people often pay less attention to the weekly, monthly, or yearly inflow of money. Instead, they watch their bank account, stock certificates, or other measures of wealth to see how quickly the desired sum is accumulated.

The specific-sum seeker often searches for simplified ways of achieving his goal. Thus, he might search for one thousand items that he can sell at a profit of $200 each. Once he finds these items he concentrates on selling them. This type of approach can be simplified to finding only one item which you can sell to one thousand customers at a certain profit per sale.

You will often recognize the specific-sum seeker by his questions about a product, process, or service and the profit it will bring him. This type of spare-time wealth builder is forever searching, seeking the one big idea that will make his fortune. You can build your wealth in the same manner, if a specific sum interests you. Many specific-sum seekers believe, like Aristotle, that "Money is a guarantee that we may have what we want in the future. Though we need nothing at the moment, it ensures the possibility of satisfying a new desire when it arises."

Some spare-time wealth builders disdain money and seek instead the ownership of something that will signify to themselves, and possibly others, the attainment of wealth. Thus, a man or woman might want to own some expensive real estate, a productive business, blue-chip stocks, a certain make of automobile, or a custom-built yacht.

To this fortune builder money is secondary, so long as he can have the object that signifies wealth to him. You may be this type of person if you have always wanted to own something on which you place a high value because of your love for it or interest in it.

Lastly, some fortune builders define wealth as the security of a certain job at a specified salary—say $100,000 a year. Others, who are less ambitious, define wealth as a job at which they need work only ten or twelve hours a week. Some people define wealth as a job that combines short hours with high pay. Take your choice of these three alternatives if you, too, define wealth as the attainment of a job having specified characteristics.

You now know a number of the ways in which people define wealth and a fortune. The next time you have a free hour, sit down and decide what wealth means to you. Have paper and pencil handy. *Write out the meaning of wealth to you.* Do this by using as few words as possible to complete the sentence: *To me wealth means* ....

FIVE STEPS TO HELP YOU DECIDE

To decide your personal meaning of wealth, you must first explore your daydreams and idle wishes for "what I'd do if I had a pile of dough." Review your hobbies and interests. Do you hunger for a round-the-world trip, a hunting lodge, membership in a country club? Or are blue-chip stocks, a business of your own, or ownership of property your main interests? List your interests on paper. Get them in written form so you can study each carefully. Having your interests in list form will show the scope of your personality as it is today. Perhaps, if your list is short, you will develop new interests that will lead to greater wealth and a more meaningful life for yourself and your loved ones. Choose that wealth interest which seems most important to you. Then write a short discussion of *why* this wealth interest is important to you, *what* the achievement of this interest means to you, and *how* you plan to achieve your objective.

If writing out the meaning of wealth disturbs you, then talk out the *why*, *what*, and *how* with your wife, husband, brother, sister, or a good friend. Should these people be unwilling to listen to you, then talk out the meaning with yourself. Just be certain to put *your* meaning of wealth into words, either written or oral. Once you decide what wealth means to you—Step 1 in choosing your wealth goal—you are ready to take Step 2.

STEP 2: DETERMINE THE COST OF YOUR WEALTH GOAL

Nothing in life is free. To achieve your defined second-income wealth goal you must work. You will probably have to give up or reduce certain activities you enjoy. If you're in your early twenties or thirties you might be willing to do without many pleasures—home, family, automobile, recreation—to achieve your desired wealth goal. An older person might be unwilling to sacrifice his comforts to chase a spare-time wealth goal. He may believe, falsely, that he has too few years left to enjoy these pleasures. The decision to seek wealth is yours—and yours alone. One of the advantages of wealth is that you can seek it at any age. For as Wynn Johnson said, "No age or time of life, no position or circumstance has a monopoly on success. Any age is the right age to start doing something."

Many natural fortune builders begin their search for wealth while teenagers. Some, like Paul Getty, became millionaires in their early twenties. Trained wealth builders are different. Many reach their fortieth birthday before they earnestly begin their search for a fortune. It takes them this long to recognize the need for and importance of wealth in their lives.

The trained wealth builder often follows an intellectual or professional career—law, engineering, science, medicine—in his earlier years. As the income from his profession begins to reach its top level, he starts to look about for additional sources of wealth. This commonly occurs at about age forty. Most intelligent people in this age range are willing to sacrifice time, energy, and pleasure to build a fortune. Why? Because, at long last, they recognize the true meaning and value of wealth.

Regardless of your background, make a "dry run" on your spare-time wealth goal. To do this try to imagine that you are working towards your goal. Visualize what you must give up to achieve this goal—Saturday-night parties, evenings at home, vacations, your favorite hobby. To determine how you would react to the loss of these pleasures, imagine yourself working while others play. Recall how your wife or husband has acted in the past while you were busy and could not devote time to her or him. Then you must decide, as objectively as possible, if you are willing to pay the price of your spare-time wealth goal.

If your answer is unequivocally *yes,* go on to Step 3. Should your answer be a doubtful *yes,* or a weak *no,* don't go on to Step 3 until you review, completely, your needs and desires. Your entire personality must seek after wealth with complete willingness; otherwise your efforts may be useless.

Never overlook the importance of the *cost* of spare-time wealth in your life. If you're willing to pay this cost your returns can be enormous. Reluctance to pay this cost may hold you back in every attempt you make. "Wealth," said the successful owner of a large mail-order company, "has its drawbacks. A man must sweat to acquire money. But once acquired, the money seems to sweeten all the effort. And once a man tastes the sweetness of his effort, he seldom gives up the heady pursuit of money."

Henry Ford began his wealth building after the age of forty and became a billionaire. Recognize the rewards that can be yours and you will be willing to pay the cost of wealth. As the famous French proverb says, "Money doesn't bring happiness, but it calms the nerves."

STEP 3: CHOOSE THE MEANS TO ACHIEVE YOUR WEALTH GOAL

Knowing what wealth and fortune mean to you, and recognizing the probable cost in personal sacrifice, puts you on the launching pad. You are ready to choose the means to achieve your spare-time wealth goal.

"But," you say, "I don't know how to achieve my wealth goal. If I did I would have reached it long ago. You wouldn't catch me reading a book on how to build a spare-time second-income fortune."

That's why this book is designed for you—to show you how to achieve your wealth goal in the quickest and easiest way possible.

To choose the *means* of achieving your wealth goal first review your past successes in earning money. List those activities—selling, teaching, writing, managing people,—which brought you more than average praise or recognition. Select from this list the activity that appeals most strongly to you and decide how you can use this activity to earn money in your spare time. If the activity isn't too easy to pinpoint, refer to the remaining chapters of this book for specific ideas—you'll find hundreds of them.

The most important result of Step 3 is isolation of the *means* you will use to acquire your wealth. With a definite means in view you are ready to apply this skill to a specific wealth-producing idea. Thus, you will be joining means and ideas. These two ingredients, backed by enthusiastic energy, should put you on the high road to real spare-time wealth and fortune. For as Emerson said, "Ideas must work through the brains and the arms of good and brave men, or they are no better than dreams." See to it that you put your money ideas into action by taking Step 4.

STEP 4: INVESTIGATE THE OPPORTUNITIES FOR ACHIEVING YOUR SPARE-TIME WEALTH GOAL

Let's say you've chosen selling as the means for building your wealth in your spare time. Investigate what branch of selling will bring you the fortune you seek. Thus, a steam-turbine salesman earns a big commission on each multi-million dollar turbine he sells. But how many turbines might he sell in a year? The automobile salesman earns much less on every car he sells, but his total annual sales income might exceed that of the turbine salesman.

How do you investigate the opportunities for achieving your spare-time wealth goal? There are many ways, including talking to people in the business and research in publications like *Dun's Review and Modern Industry* which cites specific types of business failures, profit ratios, overhead, and so forth. Government publications such as those issued by the Department of Commerce, the Small Business Administration and Federal Reserve Board are very helpful. In addition, your local public library can supply you with books on careers, earnings, opportunities, and the future of various occupations. You will also find that later chapters in this book are replete with useful ideas on earning more in your chosen activity in your spare time.

STEP 5: EVALUATE YOUR CHOSEN WEALTH GOAL

Make another "dry run." Imagine you are working and earning the money your spare-time wealth goal promises. Would you be happy? Could you withstand the pressures and tensions you would face?

Suppose the results were not what you expected. Could you shift from this wealth goal to another? Or would the commitment you made in time, energy, and money prevent you from changing? In other words, are you a flexible personality when it comes to money? Evaluate every factor concerned with your goal and yourself, using paper, pencil, notes, diagrams, statistics, and research data.

If your evaluation shows that your chosen spare-time wealth goal is for you, you are ready to begin, using the remaining chapters of this book as your guide. Should the projection show that your chosen wealth goal is unsuitable, you probably need additional help. Don't be discouraged—the remainder of this book is designed to lead you to a suitable spare-time wealth goal that will bring you the second income fortune you desire. Remember what Logan P. Smith said: "What is more mortifying than to feel that you have missed the plum for want of courage to shake the tree!"

ADVANTAGES OF CHOOSING WEALTH GOALS

Here are the stories of two men who used this five-step plan to choose their wealth goals. Study their methods to see how you, too, can choose a second-income wealth goal that will build your spare-time fortune.

Robert R., an advertising executive, wanted wealth in the form of a second income. STEP 1: He defined wealth as "A second income of $12,000 per year which I can use as I choose. The $12,000 must be free and clear after paying off any expenses related to producing the income."

STEP 2: The cost of this wealth goal, Robert R. reasoned, would be primarily in time—the time required to supervise the investment which would produce the desired income. "I'll also have to invest some of my savings," he said, "if I want to control an income-producing investment." While Robert R. disliked risking his savings he felt this was a small "cost" compared with the potential advantages of a second income of $12,000 per year. Thus, neither "cost"—time or savings risk—was unreasonable to him.

STEP 3: Next he chose the means to produce his desired income. Reviewing his past successes and interests, Robert R. concluded, "I've always been interested in rental property. My advertising experience should blend well with rental property requirements because I'll have to place ads to fill vacancies. Since my ads will be competing with others, my previous copywriting experience should be useful. Also, with the limited cash I have available, I can derive a greater income from rental property than through any other means now available to me.

STEP 4: "Now I must investigate the opportunities in rental property," Robert said. He began by reading the real estate column in his daily paper. He also studied every ad the paper carried which offered rental property for sale.

During his lunch hour he visited properties offered for sale in the area of his office. He talked to rental property owners, agents, landlords, tenants, and brokers. From these talks Robert R. built up a broad knowledge of rental property costs, profits, and operating problems. He made notes of important facts. Thus, a survey of ten properties showed his net profit for a specific cash investment would be:

Property No.	Net profit, per cent of cash investment	Cash investment
1	40	5,000
2	30	4,000
3	30	8,000
4	50	6,000
5	50	5,000
6	40	3,500
7	24	8,000
8	18	4,000
9	40	8,500
10	40	7,500

This list gave Robert R. three important facts: (1) the range in profits he could expect; (2) the range in cash investment required; (3) the expected dollar profit for a specific cash investment.

Next, Robert R. turned to helpful books on real estate investments. He studied these carefully and gleaned many useful facts about rental property purchase, operation, repair, and sale. (See later chapters for much of this money-making information.)

After thorough study of the best books, local real estate magazines, his newspaper, and actual properties offered for sale, Robert R. concluded that the opportunities offered were sufficient to fulfill his wealth goal.

STEP 5: "I must see if rental property management is completely to my liking," Robert reasoned. He sat down and went over his notes. To help analyze his findings he set up a *pro* and *con* list (*see* Chapter 2). As a guard against over-enthusiasm he listed *cons* first, *pros* second. This is the list he developed:

Disadvantages (Cons)	*Advantages (Pros)*

Disadvantages (Cons)

1. Property requires supervision
2. Apartments may be vacant for long periods
3. Maintenance costs could be high
4. Property might be difficult to sell at a later date
5. Rent controls could limit profits
6. Fires and vandalism could limit profits

Advantages (Pros)

1. Steady income from rents
2. I could prepare good rental ads
3. Rents could be collected by mail
4. An agent could operate the property for me
5. Maintenance is low in well-constructed buildings
6. Agents and building managers are readily available
7. Management and accounting are simple
8. Depreciation of the building gives tax advantages
9. Good apartments at reasonable rents are always in demand
10. Supervision of the property would require little of my time
11. The property might appreciate in value, giving me a capital gain at a later date
12. I can generate more income from rental property than from any other
13. Rental property appeals to me as an ideal source of a second income
14. I can pyramid—take income from one property to buy another—if desired
15. Rental property ownership won't interfere with my present income

Since Robert's *pros* far outweighed his *cons* he decided to use rental property to achieve his second-income fortune. Today he is a successful real estate operator in his spare time. Robert agrees with Dumas, who said, "Nothing succeeds like success." His five-step choice of a fortune goal led from successful analysis of the meaning of wealth to a profitable spare-time second income.

TURNING A PASTIME INTO A PROFIT

James K., a maintenance mechanic in a West Coast missile plant, has ten children. "My milk bill," Jim often says, "would pay some people's rent." Jim found his mechanic's salary too low to give his family the kind of life he wanted them to have. He decided to do something about it.

Jim is a beer drinker—not only because it's more economical, but also because he likes beer. One night, sitting in a San Diego tavern, he watched as the bartender deposited coin after coin in the cash register.

STEP 1: "If I only had a tavern," Jim mused, "it would give me that extra income I need." He sipped his beer. "In fact," he thought, "I'd consider myself wealthy if I had two or three profitable taverns. I will buy one—somehow. Who knows, I may become a beer baron!"

STEP 2: "I could get someone to operate the tavern during the day. That way I could still keep my missile job. For a while I'd have to tend bar at night until closing time. Sure, I'd lose some sleep—but I need only six hours now as it is. Once I get the place paid for I can hire a night man for either full- or part-time work.

"To buy a place like this would take every penny I have. I might even have to borrow a few thousand dollars. But my credit is good; I've paid off several cars on time. Though I do owe plenty on my home I have some equity in it right now. The first year would probably be tough. But I'm sure I can stand it. I've worked overtime often enough and it never seemed to hurt me." Jim finished his beer and left.

STEP 3: Jim walked home, planning his next move. "There are taverns and taverns," he said. "What I want is more than just another tavern. True, I want to sell cocktails, hard liquor, beer, and sandwiches. But what's more important, I want a tavern that people are glad to come to— a place with atmosphere. With all the Navy personnel in San Diego I could buy a tavern catering to these men. But what about civilians? They like taverns, too. And the younger crowd—the surfers, skin divers, and sailboat racing crews. What could I offer that would attract them?"

Jim spent several weeks trying to choose the *means* of accomplishing his desired objective—a tavern with atmosphere that would appeal to a large group of people. One evening, as he was mowing the lawn in front of his home the answer came to him. "I'll buy a tavern in a location that will appeal to all *three* groups," Jim said. "A place up on Pacific Beach (north of San Diego) will appeal to the surfers and the sailboat crowd. I'll decorate it with surfboards and sailboat models. A few lighted aquarium tanks with tropical fish in them will hook the skin- and scuba-divers. Some surplus life rings, ships' running lights, and a bell will help bring in the Navy crowd. And some South Sea palms, coral, and shells will attract civilians." Jim now had the *means* clearly outlined in his mind.

STEP 4: Next came a pleasant task—investigating likely taverns for possible purchase. Jim spent the next few weeks exploring taverns in the Pacific Beach and north San Diego areas. To be certain he wasn't over-looking any opportunities he also went south to National City.

Everywhere he went Jim had at least one beer. This threw his beer budget out of kilter, but it gave him time to study each tavern, its customers, rate of sales, and general physical condition.

Study of the three areas confirmed his original thought—Pacific Beach appeared to have the greatest promise. An unexpected advantage was the beach crowd—people who came to the public beaches to swim. They would form an extra group of customers. "Also," he noted happily, "there's only one hot-dog stand near the beach. That will up my food business, and should increase my profits because food, rightly handled, shows an excellent return, I've heard."

Jim roamed Pacific Beach on foot, studying each tavern in the area. One tavern, a run-down spot overlooking the ocean, caught his eye. It was midway between the surfing and bathing beaches. He studied the wooden structure from the outside and inside. True, it needed repairs, but these wouldn't be too expensive—he could paint the building himself after having a carpenter make repairs.

"The interior will take the most time," Jim said to himself as he sipped a beer. "The bar itself is in good condition. All it needs is a few coats of good gloss varnish. I can slap them on in a weekend."

Jim watched the cash register for several nights, trying to estimate the income. The nightly take didn't seem large—certainly not more than

$50. "I want a tavern that will gross at least $100 a weekday evening, and $150 on weekend evenings. I can raise the income by attracting more people to the tavern. Serving a larger glass of beer is one way of bringing the crowds in. A juke box with a full selection of surfing records will also help."

Next, Jim computed the tavern's probable current income. Using this as a guide, he compared it with taverns advertised for sale. He found that a fair price for this tavern, including the building, was about $8,000. "I'll offer the owner $9,000," Jim reasoned, "and will go to $10,000, if necessary, because I think the place has a big future in the right hands. But I won't go a dollar higher than $10,000. I could put $2500 down and pay the balance in three years out of earnings."

With his plans made, Jim obtained the name and address of the tavern owner. He was now ready to take his final step—evaluation of his spare-time wealth goal.

STEP 5: Jim made a step-by-step TO DO list and reviewed every step in it. Here's his list and projected time schedule:

1. Contact owner
2. Make $9,000 offer
3. Wait for his reaction
4. Offer $10,000, but no more, if he isn't interested
5. Close deal at $9,000 or $10,000
6. Have exterior repaired (estimated cost $500; two weeks)
7. Paint exterior (one week)
8. Varnish bar (one weekend)
9. Paint interior (two weeks)
10. Buy surplus atmosphere-gadgets (estimated cost $300; four weeks)
11. Install the atmosphere-gadgets (two weeks)
12. Continue adding gadgets, as found (six to ten weeks)
13. Increase the size of the beer stein used (one week)
14. Change the name of the tavern (one week)
15. Advertise the tavern in surfing, skin-diving, and boating magazines (three months)
16. Employ day bartender—someone with a South Seas background and appearance (two weeks)
17. Have advertising cards printed for distribution to surfing clubs, swim clubs, yacht clubs
18. Spend every evening at the tavern for six months—then hire a night man

19. Organize singing in the evening—concentrate on surfing, sea, and similar songs
20. Keep a close, daily check on income

Jim studied his "dry-run" TO DO list. It would take at least six months to get the tavern into the shape he wanted it, but he had $2,500, the probable down-payment. And, Jim remembered, Henry Ford once observed, "Money is like an arm or a leg—use it or lose it."

Jim didn't want to lose his $2,500. A low-interest bank account had little appeal. He could handle the tavern in addition to his regular job. There was no doubt about this.

Jim decided to buy the tavern. Today he is the owner of a string of taverns, each with its own brand of attractive atmosphere. His spare-time income exceeds his mechanic's income and he plans to quit his missile job soon.

FORTUNE GOALS DO PAY OFF

Recognize this fact today and you will become richer sooner. Wealth goals are the most powerful tool in your spare-time fortune-building kit.

Once you recognize the true worth of fortune goals you will begin to move towards a richer and fuller life. So begin *now*—take these five sure and proven steps towards your spare-time wealth goal:

1. *Decide* what wealth means to *you.*
2. *Determine* the cost of *your* wealth goal.
3. *Choose* the *means* to achieve *your* wealth goal.
4. *Investigate* the *opportunities* for achieving your fortune.
5. *Evaluate* your chosen fortune goal.

You are now ready for the next sure-fire key to a second-income spare-time fortune. Combining your fortune goal with the methods given in the next chapter will put you way ahead of the crowd. You will be using smart-money methods for building *your* fortune from a second income in your spare time.

Smart-money fortune builders take the fewest risks possible. Why? Because they recognize that building a fortune is a risky undertaking—even when luck is in their favor. By reducing the number of risks, the smart-money fortune builder takes some of the gamble out of his task. You, too, can use these same methods. Here are three big keys to reducing the risks in *your* spare-time second-income fortune hunt.

Key 1: Keep your present position and begin fortune-building in your spare time with a second income.

4

Use Smart-Money
Wealth-Building Methods

Many novice fortune seekers quit their jobs soon after they get a "big" idea. They start with little capital, minimum experience, much hope. Within a few months they go broke because their capital is quickly spent and there is little or no income to replace it. To reduce the number of risks in building *your* fortune, keep your job and work on the big idea in your spare time. This important key is regularly used by many successful fortune builders. The advantages of the spare-time second-income approach to your fortune are:

- No loss of your regular income.
- Your salary is a dependable source of capital.
- Mistakes aren't as damaging to your regular income.
- Fortune-buildings ideas will flow to you from your job, friends, experiences.
- You force yourself to exert maximum fortune-seeking effort.
- Your spare-time income can be reinvested because your regular income pays your living expenses. Thus, $1 of spare-time income can be worth $2 of your regular income.

EIGHT SECOND-INCOME SPARE-TIME FORTUNE BUILDERS

Does this smart-money approach really work? It surely does. Here are eight men who began their fortune-building efforts in their spare time and successfully moved into the big time:*

William Kennedy and William Box founded Box Cards while working as parking-lot attendants. They sold greeting cards of their own design by day, parked cars by night until business was good enough to permit them to devote full time to greeting cards. Their spare-time starting capital—$26.

Professor Vernon Krieble discovered *Loctite,* a sealant for holding nuts, bolts, screws, and other parts tight, while on the staff of Trinity College. Two years later he formed American Sealants Company. When he retired from teaching he devoted his full time to his booming business.

Pete Pedersen founded a bonding and insurance agency. Four years later he started a pipe-manufacturing company that proved to be a highly successful sideline. From these two businesses he went on to found Wonder Building Corp. of America, a large manufacturer of patented prefabricated buildings.

---

* Courtesy of *Fortune* Magazine; copyright by Time, Inc.

Richard Kline, while working at a movie-studio, invented a revolving-sleeve bar bell, a rowing machine, and a rubber exerciser. Setting his brother up in business, he continued working at the studio until sales rose to an acceptable level. Then he quit to form Richard Kline's Healthways of Hollywood. He has since refused an offer of $1 million for his share of the business.

Roy Brown and Arthur Grist, machine-shop supervisors at Newport News Shipbuilding & Dry Dock Co., Inc., began manufacturing windows and wall panels in a cinder-block garage, working nights and weekends. Their spare-time activities expanded to include jet-engine and missile parts and total sales of the firm soon exceeded $1 million. Today, neither Brown nor Grist works for the shipyard.

Albert Rea began collecting "finder's" commissions for locating machine tools in his spare time while studying business at Western Reserve University. Working only afternoons and Saturdays he soon branched out to buying, selling, and rebuilding machine tools. By the time he graduated he was drawing $50 per week from his spare-time venture. He then gave it his full attention and the business expanded enough to pay him over $20,000, after taxes, in his first full year.

Thousands of others who began building a fortune in their spare time have become wealthy. Many eventually quit their regular jobs to devote full time to what started as a spare-time activity. Others, preferring to continue their regular occupation, operate their spare-time business for many years. Often the business expands, showing a larger profit each year. Sometimes the spare-time business is passed along to other members of the family when the owner retires. Or the owner may sell the business at a handsome profit.

So use the first key in your fortune search—*keep your present position and begin fortune building in your spare time with a second income.* Then you will be ready to use the next key in building your fortune.

Key 2:   Use the power of leverage to multiply your wealth-building potential.

For our purposes in this book we'll define leverage as *the wealth-building power you can obtain by operating on borrowed capital, assets, or other property.* Using leverage you can appreciably expand your capital or holdings. Let's see how.

Stock market: You can buy stocks on *margin,* if you wish. Margin is the percentage of the purchase price you must pay in cash for stocks you buy, the balance being borrowed from your broker. Thus with 50% margin you can buy $1,000 worth of stock for $500 (=50% of $1,000), excluding the broker's commission. The use of a *margin account* in your stock purchases gives you leverage. In the above case you *double your purchasing power* in the stock market. With a 70% margin, you can increase your purchasing power by 30%, or almost one-third. Thus, in the stock market your leverage rises as the margin percentage decreases.

Real estate: Banks will help you finance your real estate purchases. Depending on the property, its location, and condition, you can often borrow up to 90% of the price of the real estate. This means that on a $10,000 apartment building you need put up only $1,000. Thus, you can earn a rental income on a property having a cost of ten times your investment. Your leverage is enormous—ten times your investment.

"But," you say, "I don't have $1,000, or even $100, to invest in real estate. So what good is leverage?"

Don't be discouraged. There are some sound real estate investments available offering the maximum leverage possible—i.e., *no money down.* Yes, you can buy buildings, rental property, and land without putting a penny down. Here, as you can see, your leverage is enormous because you gain control of a potentially profitable property with no investment other than time and energy.

Purchasing a business: A friend of mine recently purchased a coin-operated laundry for $24,000. His down payment was $3,000. The former owner financed the balance of $21,000. Before purchasing the laundry my friend carefully analyzed the profit potential of the business. His study showed he could pay off the $21,000 in five years, pay his rent, set aside a sum for repair and replacement of the machines, *and make a nominal profit even while paying off the loan.* Thus, for only $3,000 he acquired control of a $24,000 business which will pay for itself. His labor costs are nil, an attendant living near the laundry visits it once a day and charges only a few dollars per week for this. While my friend invested his savings in this business, he might just as easily have borrowed the $3,000 down payment. His profit would have been lower while he paid off the $3,000 loan, but leverage would have given him control of a business without his investment of a cent!

Is this deal unusual? No! There are thousands of small "absentee-owner" businesses for sale. And many will pay for themselves, if you carefully analyze the income and expenses, and use the powerful leverage of borrowed capital.

Founding a business. Most people say that finding capital for a new business is difficult. It isn't, if you know how and where to borrow money.

Have you used Key 1 and kept your job? If so, you won't have any trouble borrowing up to $5,000 on your signature from a bank. Interest rates on bank loans are moderate and you can pay off the loan in 36 months, or less, if you wish. Thus, you can get your spare-time product or service on the market without investing a penny of your own.

Suppose several banks refuse to loan you money. What then? Try a personal finance company, a business loan company, or a credit union. These firms will lend money more readily than a bank, but their interest rates may be somewhat higher. However, the interest you pay is tax deductible. High interest rates can be a burden during your first year or two of building a second-income spare-time fortune. But which would you prefer—high interest rates and a growing fortune, or zero interest payments and no second income?

LEVERAGE DO'S AND DON'TS

Leverage power, if used correctly, can multiply your wealth-building potential many times. But like too much of anything else in life, leverage can cause trouble. So, do:
- Seek the lowest interest rates and loan charges.
- Know what interest rate you are paying.
- Try to have the loan protected by low-cost life insurance.
- Get the longest payment period possible.
- Pay the smallest amount possible per month.
- Avoid loan sharks and shady operators.
- Know the exact amount of money you need.
- Carefully read the loan application *before* signing.
- Arrange a definite appointment with the loan officer.
- Plan the loan interview in advance—your reason for needing the money, and the amount needed.

- Be neatly dressed when you apply for the loan.
- Borrow only to build a second income, not to squander on passing interests.

And remember:

Don't be afraid to apply for a loan—banks *want* and *need* your business.

Don't pay loan sharks' interest rates—do without the money instead.

Don't take on high loan payments in hopes your business will grow fast.

Don't sign any loan papers until after you've read them.

Don't pay off a loan earlier if you can invest the money profitably elsewhere.

Don't miss any payments—you'll pay a late charge and your credit rating may be marred.

Don't delay final pay off of your loan. On-time pay off improves your credit rating.

You have seen how leverage can give you 100 per cent financing of a second-income business. You are now ready for Key 3.

Key 3: Keep several second-income projects going at the same time.

You gain many big, important advantages when you use Key 3. Here are a few.

With several projects going at once your statistical chances of earning big money are much higher. Multiple projects will keep you more interested and more creative; there's less chance you'll drop your second-income fortune goal because of lack of interest. You'll broaden your business experience with each new project, making you better able to turn your spare time into the most lucrative time of your day.

With income from several sources your profits will be higher. Income from one project can be used to finance another. You can pyramid —use the profits of several small businesses to build a successful big business. This is exactly what Daniel K. Ludwig, said to be worth more than $500 million, did. Starting with a bank loan of $5,000, he invested in some secondhand tugboats and barges. After repairing them, he chartered them to various operators. Profits from this small beginning allowed him to invest in ocean-going vessels, mainly oil tankers and bulk carriers. Another bank loan allowed him to expand and modernize his fleet. The fleet grew until it was considered the largest in the world owned by an individual.

HINTS FOR PROFITABLE PYRAMIDING

Your pyramiding may never approach Ludwig's. But you can, with a small beginning, build a second-income spare-time fortune that will make your life more comfortable and more secure. Here are some useful hints for successful pyramiding of your second income:

1. Don't drain away business income for non-business (pleasure) purposes. Such tactics cripple the growth of your second-income fortune.
2. Be patient—fortunes are seldom built in a day.
3. Leave your money in profitable projects. Take it out of unprofitable ones.
4. Always seek large, steady profits. Never be satisfied with marginal, time-consuming projects that deliver low profits.
5. Expand your activities. Ludwig expanded and diversified from shipping to oil refining, orange groves, hotels, dredging, coal mines, real estate, shipyards, a cattle ranch, and many other interests. You can also expand, feeding profits from one activity to another.
6. Try to be objective about every project. Don't lose money on any project, even one having strong sentimental appeal to you.
7. Build your business pyramid towards a specific fortune goal (Chapter 2).
8. Never be afraid to start a new pyramid after another reaches its top profit potential.

MANAGING MULTIPLE PROJECTS

Today, you probably work five days a week. What do you do during your two days off? "Relax," you'll probably say. "By the time Friday night comes around I'm so bushed it takes me two days to recover."

Is this really so? Doesn't a long sleep Saturday morning put you back in shape? What about that weekend last summer when you had an exciting trip planned? Didn't you get up early both days and enjoy yourself thoroughly? Sure you did.

Now suppose you found earning a second income just as exciting as that trip. Wouldn't you be willing to devote some of your spare time to earning the extra money?

Look at it this way. If you work ten hours per week in your spare time you can earn up to $1,000 per week, depending on your hourly rate. Let's say you start at a low rate and build to a high hourly rate. Here's what your weekly spare-time second income could be:

Hourly rate for spare-time work	Weekly income if you work 10 hours per week
$ 0.50	$ 5.00
1.00	10.00
2.00	20.00
2.50	25.00
5.00	50.00
7.50	75.00
10.00	100.00
20.00	200.00
50.00	500.00
75.00	750.00
100.00	1,000.00

Many people start at less than $1.00 per hour spare-time income and build this to $25 or more per hour. What is their secret? It is this: *They are willing to start at a low hourly rate because they believe that with some extra income they can pyramid it to a high hourly income by having several second-income projects going at once.* So don't be afraid to start. You stand to lose very little, if you faithfully apply Keys 1, 2, and 3.

ONE MAN'S EXPERIENCE

Earlier I told you that I'm a "boat nut." I started my career as an engineer. While piloting my cabin cruiser I often had to figure how far my boat would go in a certain time. On a pitching boat this isn't easy to do. So I designed a simple calculator that allowed me to get a quick, accurate answer to the distance problem. In designing this calculator I used my engineering experience to develop the simplest form possible.

When my boating friends saw the calculator they immediately wanted copies for themselves. Soon I developed nineteen other simple, easy-to-use boating calculators. They are now sold all over the world, through boating supply stores, mail order, and by direct solicitation. These products are copyrighted and can be sold exclusively by my company for the next 50 years. Since I spent only a few hours preparing each, and the manufacturing cost is moderate, my hourly return is extremely high.

And here's an interesting sidelight: Many of these calculators were published in boating magazines *before* I made them into products. The magazines paid me for each calculator. Income from the magazines alone exceeded $10 per hour. And I'll be selling these calculators for the next 50 years. Can anyone lose on a second-income deal like this?

While developing the calculators I continued working on several other projects. These included books such as the one you are now reading, magazine articles, teaching evening college classes, industrial consulting, and research in the boating and marine fields. My income thus comes from many sources. Should one source cease, there are several others which will help me continue my pyramiding.

What is the big secret of successfully managing your multiple projects? It is this: *Devote some time to each project but once a project is earning a profit, give it as little time as possible.*

Seek projects requiring the minimum amount of supervision time. Typical projects of this type are "absentee-management" stores, real estate, gas stations, and similar businesses. You hire a manager, agent, superintendent, or other employee who runs the business for you. Once a week, or less frequently depending on the business, you stop by to pick up the income and take it to the bank. By pyramiding you can develop a string of stores or other businesses. You can devote Saturday morning or one evening a week to collecting the income from your places of business.

Other minimum-supervision second-income projects you might consider include coin-operated laundries, taverns, travel agencies, professional consulting in a field of specialized knowledge, lecturing for local civic or educational groups, book authorship, and ownership of facilities catering to specific age groups. Here are two interesting examples of such projects:

Michael DeZutter, manager and developer of many outstanding country and dining clubs, also served as a technical consultant on the planning and building of exclusive clubs. Thus, he used his knowledge of clubs as a basis for his consulting service. His service was so specialized that clients sought him out from all over the world. His consulting work did not interfere with his other activities.

In Paris, France, Henri Leproux runs a dance hall for French teen-agers. As many as 1,000 teen-agers crowd his *Golf Drout* in one evening. The teen-agers regard his hall as their personal club. Some of the young people volunteer to sing for their friends. Mr. Leproux, with a keen ear for good music, brings the talented singers to the French recording companies. Today a number of the popular younger singers and singing groups in France owe their start to Mr. Leproux. Some of these singers still return to the *Golf Drout* to ask Mr. Leproux' advice about their careers and song choices. The finding and developing of these young singers do not interfere with Mr. Leproux' activities in the *Golf Drout*.

You *can* find a number of profitable projects to build your spare-time second income. Begin by deciding what you like to do best and how you can turn this interest into a product or service others will buy. Then once you have your first project showing a profit, go on to the second, and the third, fourth, fifth. Bear in mind, at all times, Key 3: *Keep several spare-time second-income projects going at the same time.*

BUILD YOUR CREATIVITY WITH MULTIPLE PROJECTS

Some beginning, spare-time second-income fortune builders complain that multiple projects are "too much work." This may or may not be true when you first start. If you choose projects closely akin to your interests in life the work will never seem to be a burden. The reason for this is that you will enjoy what you're doing. Time will pass quickly. And when the profits start coming in you will enjoy them so much that you'll work harder to increase them. Having a spare-time second income can give you the greatest feeling of freedom and independence you've ever had.

What's more, with multiple projects your mind will teem with ideas. A decision you make for one project will spark an idea for another. You will live at a higher pitch, your interest in life will be greater because the multiple projects are building your fortune and future. Furthermore, the more creative you become the greater are your chances for developing an important idea that will lead you to real prosperity.

Creative thinking is the biggest asset you can have to build a lucrative second income. Since multiple, spare-time second-income projects assist you in developing your creative abilities, you can't lose when you keep several projects going at once. Try it and see.

TAX ADVANTAGES OF MULTIPLE PROJECTS

Many spare-time second-income fortune builders operate their multiple projects under one company name. Few of these are corporations; most are *sole proprietorships*, i.e., a company registered with the county or state clerk and owned by one person. The cost of setting up a sole proprietorship is nominal. For example, New York State charges only $5.00 to register the company. By comparison, it costs about $500 to form a corporation in New York State.

In a sole proprietorship which operates several related projects, the various business expenses can be deducted separately for each project. Thus, labor, maintenance, supplies, rent, light, heat, depreciation, taxes, commissions, bad debts, and so on, can be entered on Schedule C of your income tax form. With careful planning and good tax advice you can obtain the maximum legal deductions to which you are entitled. With maximum deductions, your after-tax income is greater; you retain more of the money you earn.

Smart-money fortune builders recognize the tax advantages of multiple projects. Obtain wise tax advice and you, too, can build a spare-time second-income fortune for yourself and your family.

In Chapter 4 we took a look at the power of leverage and how you can use it in your spare-time search for a fortune. Now you are ready to examine more closely some specific financing techniques you might use. Read this chapter carefully, for you will certainly find many profitable techniques in it.

5

You have probably heard of many businesses, founded on a shoestring, that grew into corporate giants. This kind of beginning was easier fifty years ago than it is today. Modern business requires capital.

Finance Your Way

to a Fortune

When you don't have the capital, or prefer to retain your own funds, you need financing. Good financing is important if you want your business to prosper.

Why is good financing important in building a second-income fortune in your spare time? Here are five major reasons:

- Good financing allows you to take advantage of profit opportunities.
- Money can help you find and develop profitable projects.
- Adequate financing gives you more freedom to act when you find a profitable project.
- Capital releases you from fears of unpaid bills and lost profit opportunities.
- Sufficient funds give you an independent outlook and stimulate your creativity.

To convince yourself of the truth of these principles, think of the last time you had a sizeable sum of money in the bank. Didn't it give you feelings of power, strength, independence, and confidence when you thought of the money? Certainly it did. Having adequate financing for your spare-time second-income business will increase your chances for outstanding success because you will have similar feelings about the business.

YOU CAN GET BY WITH LITTLE CAPITAL

In Chapter 4 you saw how an absentee-owner or minimum-supervision type of business opens the paths to successful pyramiding. Now you will see how you can get by with little capital in your second-income business.

Different businesses, as you've probably sensed, require varying amounts of starting capital. Thus, if you wanted to drive a taxicab in your spare time you might invest $3,000 or $4,000 in a new cab. Then you'd have to pay a fee for the hack license. Your insurance might cost another $1,000, or so. The total investment could amount to $5,000 or more, depending on your location, type of cab purchased, and other factors. You could make a fairly accurate prediction, before you bought the cab, of what your second income would be, based on the number of hours worked per day and the fares you would collect. With this information in hand you could decide whether the cab business was a wise investment.

What has your study shown? It has revealed how much starting capital you will need. If you study a number of businesses you will probably find that some require ten or more times as much capital as others. We'll call the business requiring little capital a *low-capital project*. The large-capital business we'll call a *high-capital project*.

Now, are high-capital projects more profitable than low-capital projects? Not always. Then why do some people invest in high-capital projects? The answer to this varies, but the usual reason is that certain people enjoy working on high-capital projects. Many of these people have sufficient starting capital to invest in high-capital projects. Sometimes this money was earned in successful low-capital projects. Here are five useful facts about low-capital projects:

Fact 1: Low-capital projects are your best starting point for building a second-income spare-time fortune.

Fact 2: Low-capital projects can bring you rewarding profits, in dollars per hour of working time.

Fact 3: Low-capital projects usually involve less of your time and efforts in non-productive activities like maintenance of equipment, complicated insurance arrangements, title searches and the like.

Fact 4: Low-capital projects absorb less of your profits, allowing you to pyramid faster and more profitably.

Fact 5: Low-capital projects usually require less floor space, machinery, and other equipment.

Most fortune builders begin with low-capital projects and later switch to high-capital projects. For the present, let's concentrate on getting you started in one or more low-capital projects.

SEEK LOW-CAPITAL PROJECTS

What are the characteristics of low-capital projects? Usually they are: a small initial investment for supplies; no need for a formal place of business; most sales activities conducted by mail; trucks, warehouses, production machinery, and large numbers of skilled workers not needed; legal aspects of the business are relatively simple.

Where can you find a low-capital business? Chapter 9 lists many profitable businesses of this type. If you apply the five characteristics given above to any business you are considering you will quickly learn if it is the low-capital type. Here is a short checklist you will find useful in evaluating every business you are considering. With the resulting data, you can easily find how much starting capital you need for each business that interests you. Then you will be ready to finance your way to a fortune.

Business Analysis Checklist

1. Type of business:_____
2. Capital required: $_____
3. Probable income, $ per hr: At start:_____Later:_____
4. Time required, hr per day:_____
5. Floor space required, sq ft:_____
6. No. of employees required:_____
7. Cost of machinery and equipment:_____
8. Primary sales outlets:_____
9. Business advantages:_____
10. Business disadvantages:_____

Some beginning spare-time fortune builders doubt that a lucrative business can be built on borrowed capital. If you are one of these, consider the firm Parcel Tankers, Inc. At the time of the writing of this book the ten-ship Parcel firm specialized in carrying "anything liquid"—from chemicals to molasses. The firm was started on a sum of $23,000, of which $17,000 was borrowed. Four years later its capital was $750,000, and its revenues came to about $8 million. One key to the firm's success is that it operates a scheduled tanker service where none existed before. The rates charged by the firm are less than half those charged before the firm was formed.

NINE STEPS TO SURE-FIRE BANK FINANCING

You can borrow money from banks in a number of ways—personal loans, short-term loans, revolving credit, business loans, and home refinance loans. Any of these can help you finance your way to a fortune, if you use the proper approach in applying for your loan. Here are nine steps you can use for any type of loan.

1. *Decide how much money you need.* Use the Business Analysis

Checklist as a guide. Where possible, try to limit your loan request to $5,000, or less.

2. *Check your local newspapers for advertisements of banks seeking to loan funds.* When a bank runs an ad of this type it usually means that excess funds are available. The ad may appear in any number of forms, including "Personal Loans," "Business Loans," "Executive Loans," or "Educational Loans." In general, your best chance for quick approval of a loan is in the bank where you have your checking and savings accounts. The next best is in a bank that advertises loans. In some cases the bank having your checking and savings accounts may not make loans. In other cases you may prefer to keep your loan and bank accounts at separate banks.

3. *Obtain a loan application* by visiting, calling, or writing the bank.

4. *Fill out the application.* Keep several facts in mind when filling out the application: (a) If you have large installment debts (for your car, home, or medical expenses) you should pay off all these debts, except your home, before taking on another loan payment. (b) Most banks look more favorably on applicants who have been with one firm for more than a year, have lived at the same address for more than a year, and own their home. (c) When you give the purpose of your loan as "payment of taxes" or a similar purpose you will generally be required to pay the loan off in one year or less, because within a year you will probably face a new tax bill.

5. *Consult with the bank's loan officer* if you have difficulty with any part of the application. Carefully point out to him that you are not applying for the loan at this time, you are only seeking help with the application.

6. *Be continually alert* while talking to the loan officer. Remember: *He wants your business; he is on your side. If he makes a wise loan it benefits the bank's business and his own reputation.* So you will find most loan officers anxious to assist you. While studying your application the loan officer may make certain indirect comments to you, such as: "Do you really think your house (or car) is worth only this much?" Or "Don't you have some other income you may have overlooked?" These and similar comments are designed to assist you in preparing a more acceptable application. The loan officer cannot, however, make any changes in your application—your loan request stands or falls on the facts you supply.

7. *Take care to have an acceptable reason* for needing the money. Here again the loan officer can be very helpful. If you are unsure of your reason, leave the "Purpose" space blank. Tell the loan officer in general terms what you wish to do with the money. He may answer you this way: "We'd be happy to lend you $5,000 to pay off some outstanding bills. If you have some money left over I suppose you could invest it in this spare-time business you're talking about. But we'd much prefer to lend money for paying off bills." This is your cue that the application will probably be turned down unless you use the purpose suggested (payment of bills, in this example). There's nothing to prevent you from acquiring some *business* bills before you obtain the loan. Then you are not being dishonest when you use this purpose on your application.

8. *Make an appointment* to submit the application in the next day or so. Having an appointment ensures you the attention your loan needs. Also, the loan officer looks on you more favorably than someone who strolls in off the street. In borrowing money for a number of businesses I have personally found that two visits are better than one. Loan officers are human, and they feel more comfortable with you on the second visit. Since the loan officer's opinion of you and your loan is an important factor in the final approval, being on friendly terms increases your chances of acceptance.

9. *Say as little as possible during the loan interview.* Many an over-talkative applicant has talked himself right out of a loan. Answer every question the loan officer asks truthfully and accurately. Stop when you've given the information he requests.

INVESTIGATE OTHER FORMS OF BANK FINANCING

Most beginning part-time fortune builders limit their thinking to bank loans in which the full amount is received in one payment from the bank. While this is the most common type of loan, there are other arrangements you should consider. Here are a few. In each, the loan application and the procedure to follow are similar to those just described.

Revolving credit. Sometimes called "instant money," revolving credit consists of having a loan for a specific sum, say $5,000, approved by a bank. The bank reserves this money in your name. You can write checks for any sum up to $5,000 and the bank will honor them. One month later you begin repaying the bank. Depending on the agreement you have with the bank, the sum borrowed may be repaid in one month, or over a period of several months or years. The usual interest charge is 1 per cent of the unpaid balance per month.

Revolving credit has a number of advantages for the part-time fortune builder. You pay interest only on the money you use. Once the loan application is approved, you know that you have a certain sum available for use at all times, without having to re-apply at the bank. Should your project require a smaller investment than you estimated, you have the choice of using the money on another project or leaving it in the bank.

Line of credit. This is similar to revolving credit. The bank agrees to honor checks up to a certain sum. You are usually required, however, to *clean up*—that is, pay up any amount you owe the bank at least once a year. This may strain your capital sources when you are first beginning.

Some banks require a *compensating balance* for your line of credit. The compensating balance is a sum you are required to keep on deposit in the bank at all times while your line of credit is in force. Most banks require a compensating balance of at least 20 per cent of the amount of the line of credit. Thus, with a $10,000 line of credit you would be required to keep $2,000 on deposit, leaving $8,000 available to you.

Shrewd second-income fortune builders sometimes borrow the amount needed for the compensating balance. The lender, a bank or firm other than the bank extending the line of credit, usually charges low interest rates—often only 0.75 per cent—because the money is known to be on deposit. The compensating balance does not draw interest. With this arrangement you have use of the full amount of your line of credit. You do, of course, have the extra interest charge on the $2,000 compensating balance you borrowed. However, if you invest your money so that it *earns* money, the interest charge is not burdensome.

"Balloon" loans. In these you make relatively small monthly payments for the life of the loan, except that your last payment is a large one. Let's say you borrow $2,400 for twelve months. With an ordinary bank loan your monthly repayment would be about $210 for twelve months. With a balloon loan you might pay $10 per month for eleven months. The twelfth payment would be $2,410—the $2,400 principal, plus the interest for the last month.

A balloon loan has the distinct advantage of giving you full use of the borrowed money for almost the entire duration of the loan. In an ordinary loan you have full use of the amount borrowed for only one month; after that you have less of the principal each month because every payment contains part of the principal. A balloon loan has the distinct *disadvantage* of a large final payment.

Some smart-money borrowers use balloon loans to build their second-income fortunes. Should they be unable to make the final balloon payment, these fortune builders simply refinance—that is, they sign a new application (also called a *note*) for the amount of the principal. They then go through another twelve month or longer period during which they pay only interest. Eventually, of course, the balloon must be paid. But some farsighted borrowers will refinance a balloon again and again, until their investment earns enough to pay off the balloon.

Multiple bank loans. Some experienced second-income fortune builders borrow from several banks when one bank is unwilling to furnish all the capital needed, or will not approve the lending period the borrower desires. While this technique is safe for experienced fortune builders, you should avoid using it during your early ventures. Why? Because you can quickly spend the money obtained from several loans and be deeply in debt before your investment begins to show a profit.

Multiple bank loans are also used for annual cleanup of lines of credit. Thus, if you have three lines of credit you might use the first two for working capital. The third is inactive until you must clean up the first two. Then you take funds from the third line of credit and pay off the first two. A few months later you borrow from the first or second to pay the third. This technique provides a steady flow of funds and enables you to retain a high credit standing with each bank. You must, of course, have a steady income of some kind to furnish the money needed for interest payments. You can, if you wish, also use multiple bank loans to pay off personal or business loans in the same way as described for lines of credit. Here, again, you must use caution not to overburden yourself with large payments.

Ninety-day pay loans. With these loans you make no payments for the first ninety days after receiving your cash from the bank. When you have a second-income project that will pay off quickly, this type of loan frees you from making any payments for three months. During this time your project may generate enough profit to pay back all or a large part of the loan.

Do not be deceived by the ninety-day pay loan—you *are* charged interest on the full amount of the loan during this payment-free period. The greatest advantage of this type of loan is the breathing spell it gives you during the first three months when no payments are required.

Commercial loans. Sometimes called "standing" loans by banks, this type has definite attractions. Here you borrow a specific sum for three months, six months, or a year for business purposes. During the life of the loan you make no installment payments. When the loan becomes due you are expected to pay the full amount, plus interest. Thus, you are free to use the full amount of the loan in your business for the duration of the time period.

Suppose you cannot pay the full amount when the loan falls due. What happens? Most banks will allow you to take either of two steps: (1) Make an interest payment for the period involved and *renew* the loan —in effect, extend the loan for another six or twelve months, depending on your needs. Once again, after paying the nominal interest charge, you will be free of monthly installment payments. (2) Pay off part of the principal and renew the balance for another six or twelve months. Again, you will be free of installment payments. The true interest rate on a commercial loan is lower than on a personal loan because you have use of the entire loan amount for the full period of the loan. With a personal loan, which you repay in monthly installments, you have an average of only half the loan amount for the full period.

Other types of loans. There are at least two dozen other types of loans you might obtain from your bank. These include secured, passbook, bond and stock, accounts receivable, chattel mortgage, warehouse, insurance, and numerous other types of loans. The best way to learn about these is to visit your local bank and make friends with the loan officer. You'll find him friendly, alert, and informed. He loves to talk about money. You can learn much from him.

Tell him about your desire to build a second-income fortune in your spare time. He'll be sympathetic and will probably make many useful suggestions. You may find that he will become the most important person in your life because he controls one of your sources of capital. A preliminary discussion such as this will often pave the way for future loans that are made quickly and easily.

Dr. Herbert Axelrod, founder of T.F.H. Publications, Inc., largest publisher for tropical fish hobbyists, began publishing pamphlets for fish fanciers in his spare time. When he decided to expand his publishing activities, a $25,000 bank loan was an important factor in the outstanding success he achieved and enjoys today. When your opportunity becomes available a bank loan may mean the difference between success and failure.

Capital and leverage pay off. A little capital can go a long way if you have leverage. Various authorities estimate that it costs $18,000 today to provide one new job in industry. You can develop a part-time job for yourself with much less money, if you use the financial facilities of a good bank and the leverage opportunities open to alert fortune builders. Everyone who has ever built a fortune combined capital and leverage. Remember: leverage and a little capital can produce big profits for you.

Don't be penalized by high interest rates. You need not worry about high interest rates when you borrow from a bank, *except* when you must refinance a loan before you repay it. The need to refinance a loan can occur when you find that you cannot meet the payments. In refinancing you bring your previous loan up to its former level, or a higher level. Either way, your interest costs can skyrocket, compared to the rate for a regular loan. In some cases the true annual interest rate can approach fifty percent.

If you must refinance a loan, the best course to follow would be to go to another bank and obtain a loan for the actual cash you would get out of refinancing your previous loan. Use this cash to pay off part of the previous loan. This will give you several months during which you are free of large monthly payments. Also, your true interest charges will be only about one-third the amount on a refinanced loan.

Guard your credit rating. Take every step necessary to repay your loan on time. Your credit rating is a valuable asset in the search for a spare-time second-income fortune. If you do not have a previously established credit rating, your bank loan officer can help you develop one. To do this he may ask you to take a small loan and repay it quickly. Follow his advice. Guard your credit rating at all times by making full installment payments *on time*.

CONSIDER A PRIVATE STOCK OFFERING

Bank loans of various kinds are probably your best source of funds when you are starting your second-income business. However, you may find that you need more capital than banks are willing to lend, or the repayment period may be too short for you to show a large enough profit to pay off the loan. When this happens, consider a private stock offering or, as it is sometimes called, a private placement.

For best results with a private offering, select your second-income spare-time fortune business from among those requiring minimum capital. Many businesses of this type are discussed in Chapter 9. Then, if you offer stock to *less than twenty-five buyers*, your stock offering will, in most states, be termed a private placement. A private placement usually need not be registered with the United States Securities and Exchange Commission. This relieves you of much paper work.

You can make a private placement by selling shares of stock to your friends and relatives. If you can find twenty-four people who will each purchase $1,000 worth of stock your corporation will have $24,000 capital to start. Or if each stockholder buys $100 worth of stock you will have $2,400. In general, it is wiser to seek more starting capital than you estimate you need because the extra money can almost always be used during the first few months before profits are earned.

Money obtained by selling stock is called *equity capital* because the stockholder owns part of the corporation by reason of the shares he holds. Capital obtained from bank loans must be repaid within a given period and a specified rate of interest is charged. Capital obtained from the private sale of stock need not be repaid within any specified time period. Also, you are not required to pay interest for the use of the money. You *are* required, however, to make the best effort possible to have your firm earn a profit and prosper so the stockholders' equity will increase.

A private placement is possible, if you are an experienced businessman. On the other hand, if you are starting your first second-income business without previous experience, you would probably be safer using a bank loan or other forms of financing. Once you have broadened your business experience and have a proven profit-making ability you can consider, and use, a private placement.

PUBLIC STOCK OFFERINGS PROVIDE BIG CAPITAL

Many Regulation A stock offerings ($300,000 or less stock sold to the general public) are successfully made by part-time fortune builders.

Such offerings require more experience and judgment than usually possessed by beginning fortune builders. Therefore, the procedures and methods you should use are presented later in this book in Chapter 11. By the time you read that chapter you will be better equipped to follow and use the many pointers given there.

FACTORING CAN MULTIPLY YOUR CASH

Once you have steady customers for your business you might consider factoring, if your income fluctuates because your customers do not pay according to a predictable schedule.

In working with a factor you sell him your *receivables* (bills owed you for products or services) and he collects the money due. You receive immediate cash from the factor for the receivables. Thus, you need not wait ninety days or more to collect the payments for your services. The factor assumes the risk for bad-debt losses. A factor, of course, must make a profit for his services. He will charge you between six and ten per cent per year of your receivables to collect them. As the amount of your receivables increases, the factor's fee percentage will proportionately decrease.

Factoring can give you a steady cash income if you make regular sales of your products or services. Since many factors set a lower limit on the annual receivables they will handle (for example, $100,000) you may have to spend some time looking for a factor who will handle your account. There are, however, factors who specialize in small accounts. Their fees may be somewhat higher than those cited if your customers are poor credit risks.

Factoring is growing in popularity. At one time, factoring was confined almost solely to bankrupt firms. Today, more and more successful small firms regularly use factors. You must, of course, still be able to show a profit *after* the factor deducts his charge. For the first few years, while you are building your second-income fortune, you will probably be better off using the principles given in a good book on credits and collections. Once your business is solidly established you can turn your receivables over to a factor. Since you will then be free of the chore of preparing and collecting bills, you can devote more time to developing new and profitable businesses.

SALE AND LEASEBACK CAN GENERATE CASH

Suppose you own some real estate—a building, or other property you plan to use in your business—but you lack cash with which to start the business. Sale and leaseback of the property may permit you to finance your way to a second-income fortune. Here's what you would do.

Find a buyer for your property by advertising in newspapers and magazines. Insist that the buyer purchase the property outright for cash and then lease it to you for a specified period. The buyer can obtain most of his cash purchase price through a bank or savings and loan mortgage.

Sale and leaseback has several advantages for you. This procedure will give you cash which is taxed at the lower capital-gains rate. The lease guarantees you use of the property, and your rent for the property is fully deductible on your income tax. If you held the property and used it in your business you could deduct only depreciation of the building and other equipment, real-estate taxes, and maintenance expenses. The total of these is usually less than the rent. Further, you are freed of maintenance expenses on the property, giving you more cash for business operation. Finally, the stimulus of your second-income fortune can make you more creative, leading you to find profitable use for property that is currently idle.

SELLING BEFORE YOU BUY IMPROVES YOUR CASH POSITION

Ingenious spare-time second-income fortune builders sometimes manage to sell a product, property, or service *before* they buy it. Thus, when they are ready to pay for the item they are already holding checks for the sale of all or part of the item. Should you use this arrangement you'll find that you need very little cash to operate your business.

Let's say you are interested in speculating in raw and improved land as a means of earning a part-time income. You find a piece of land on a highway and, after study and thought, decide it has excellent possibilities for sub-division. You contact the owner and negotiate a mutually agreeable price. You offer the owner a nominal amount of money for a 15-day *option* to buy the land. An option is a contract giving you the right to purchase the land at the agreed upon price within the agreed upon time (in this case 15 days). During this time the owner agrees not to sell the land to anyone else, even at a higher price. Should you decide not to buy the land within the time limit (15 days), the owner keeps your deposit (say $100).

You now have 15 days in which to sell all or part of your land. If you are ingenious, observant, and have a wide circle of friends, you may be able to sell the land for more than you plan to pay for it *before* you complete the purchase. Many second-income spare-time fortune builders specialize in deals like this. To be successful you must be constantly alert to the needs of others. Also, you must be able to judge a piece of property not on the basis of what it is today but on what it *could be* in the future.

A friend of mine, Jack G., speculates in Liberty ships, C-2 cargo ships, and T-2 tankers in his spare time. These vessels were widely used in World War II. Today many of them are being sold for scrap at prices in the $100,000 to $200,000 range. Every time a shortage of shipping develops, the price a shipping company is willing to pay for one of these ships jumps. So Jack G. reads his morning and evening newspapers with an eye to national and international developments.

Thus, when Canada began selling wheat to Russia, Jack took options on two Liberty ships. His purchase price was to be $125,000. When the Russian wheat sale was approved by Congress, Jack received offers of $225,000 apiece for his ships. This is a price appreciation of 80 per cent per ship. Jack, of course, is an experienced businessman who closely follows every development that might affect his spare-time shipping interests. Today he probably knows almost as much about the recent Communist agricultural crisis as he does about ships and shipping. His option cost on ships is always low compared to the final sale price.

Selling before you buy has many advantages for the second-income spare-time fortune builder. Your investment is nominal. The possibility of loss of your option deposit stimulates your creativity and makes your efforts more effective. Realizing that your second income depends on bringing a need and a source together, you become more alert for profitable situations. You can easily switch from one field of activity to another; you do not need a license or any other kind of official approval.

SBIC'S—UNTAPPED CAPITAL SOURCES

In 1958 Congress approved the creation of Small Business Investment Companies to help finance small businesses of all kinds. A Small Business

Investment Company (SBIC) is licensed and supervised by the Small Business Administration (SBA). An SBIC can lend you money for your business. The loan can run for five to twenty years, depending on the amount and the arrangements made between yourself and the SBIC. Interest rates are subject to SBA and state rules. In general, the rates are competitive with other sources of capital. If you operate your spare-time business as a corporation, an SBIC can, if it wishes, purchase common stock or convertible debentures (bonds) as a means of supplying cash to you. In every case the SBIC makes its own decisions as to which investments it will make, and in what form—loan, stock, or debentures.

The SBIC is important to you from two aspects: (1) as a source of capital, and (2) as a potential business in which you might make a spare-time fortune. Almost every one of the nearly 1,000 SBIC's in existence today was formed by a group of businessmen as a second-income source.

To find an SBIC that might lend you money for your business, study the "Capital to Invest" columns of your local newspaper, *The Wall Street Journal*, *The New York Times*, and similar publications. The loan requirements vary widely from one SBIC to another. So don't be discouraged if the first few SBICs turn you down. Keep trying; the next SBIC you visit may be looking for a business just like yours in which it can invest some money. The other aspect of SBIC's—operation as a business—is discussed later in this chapter.

THREE OVERLOOKED CAPITAL SOURCES

Venture-capital firms are a promising source of capital for new businesses. The venture-capital firm is usually composed of individuals seeking to invest their pooled capital in promising enterprises. Most venture-capital firms will take much higher risks than an SBIC. In fact, with some venture-capital firms all you need is a good idea and they will put you into business. For such backing the firm will want at least a 60 per cent share in your organization. While you may balk at giving away this much of your profit, 40 per cent of the total profit is better than no profit at all.

Insurance companies will often lend money to a small business at 6 per cent interest. Check with your own insurance company; it may have a small-business loan department. If so, inquire about the types of loans available. You may find that your insurance company will be delighted to lend you all the money you need at a nominal interest rate.

Finance companies in your town or state are another overlooked source of business capital. Many finance companies will accept a loan application that the average bank will decline.

＇ When dealing with any financial organization, follow the general hints given earlier in this chapter. Never expect to have a loan application approved unless you have fully prepared yourself in advance of the interview.

USE THESE SMART-MONEY CAPITAL-RAISING METHODS

In seeking financing for your business you are looking for but one item—money. Many smart-money, spare-time fortune builders, realizing this from the beginning of their efforts, get into the "money business" first. What is the money business? It is any activity in which money is the principal product offered. Thus, many smart-money fortune builders form SBIC's, buy banks, operate home loan and savings associations, run finance companies, and engage in other similar activities where money is the primary product—all in their spare time. "But," you say, "the money these people control is not theirs." True. Yet having money sources available to you makes it easier for you to meet people who are looking for a sound way to invest their money. Once you become friendly with people who have money to invest—and there are many more than you may think —you have an excellent chance of obtaining financing for your second-income spare-time fortune. Or, better yet, your money business may make your fortune. Let's see how others use this technique.

SBIC formation. Of the nearly 1,000 SBIC's operating at the time of this writing, most are run by people having other business interests. Some of these people have dropped their other business activities to devote full time to their SBIC, others continue their multiple business interests.

Thus, a recent *Wall Street Journal* article reports a number of interesting SBIC financing arrangements. Here are a few, *all perfectly legal.**

1. The sole owner of a plumbing and heating company, who is also vice president and secretary of an SBIC, borrowed $75,000 for ten years from his SBIC to purchase a new building for his plumbing company.

---

* Courtesy of and copyright by *The Wall Street Journal.*

The terms of the loan were more favorable than he could obtain at a bank. His investment in the SBIC is $50,000.

2. A dealer in real estate and other ventures, who is also a stockholder and director of an SBIC, is the owner of an investment counseling firm which was granted a contract to manage this SBIC. The SBIC, at the time of the *Journal* article, had invested $106,000, more than a third of its capital, in two companies in which the director became an investor. One company operates a timber farm; the other markets art replicas. The SBIC director is also president of the art company.

3. The president of an SBIC is also a stockholder and trustee of an apartment house. His SBIC took a third mortgage on the apartment house at a 10 per cent interest rate, which is somewhat lower than the rate charged other borrowers by this SBIC.

4. Another SBIC president operates a real estate firm and the SBIC within one office. He is also president of the real estate firm. Besides these two activities, he sells insurance and owns a liquor store. His clerk (secretary), who is also a director of this SBIC, is treasurer of a realty corporation that received a $17,500 loan from the SBIC. A $30,000 loan was granted on a nursing home of which the son of the clerk of the SBIC was an incorporator. The SBIC received stock for half ownership of the nursing home corporation.

These and many other instances show that formation of an SBIC can lead you to productive capital sources. You probably cannot form an SBIC yourself because a minimum capital of $300,000 is required. But you can be one of several founders or stockholders for only a few thousand dollars. The resulting financing you may obtain, either outside the SBIC, or within it, plus the growth of your investment in the SBIC, can make the venture highly profitable.

Before making any financial arrangements with an SBIC, remember that the SBA applies three criteria to loan applications: (a) There must be non-interested persons in the SBIC with power to block the transaction. (b) The terms must be "fair and reasonable." (c) The arrangement must "serve the purposes of the Small Business Investment Act of 1958."

Small-town banks. Thousands of small-town banks are offered for sale during your lifetime. These banks are often sold at nominal prices. Owning such a bank can be a profitable sideline, as well as a source of ideas for raising capital.

As a banker you are allowed to invest a portion of the bank's funds to generate income. The investments might be in mortgages, in loans to businessmen, personal loans, and similar approved activities. Should your spare-time business need money, it is conceivable that the board of directors of the bank would approve your loan application whereas another bank might turn you down.

Check the business columns of your local paper if you live in a small town. Obtain copies of small-town papers if you live in a large city. Watch for advertisements of banks for sale.

Home loan associations. It has been said that the charter for a home loan and savings association in a certain western state is worth $1 million. Yet obtaining a charter is not expensive. While you must have capital to begin business as a savings and loan association, this capital is often obtained from friends, relatives, and investors interested in expanding their income.

Check mortgage practices in your local area before considering formation of an association of this type. If second and third mortgages are common, you have a good chance of opening a successful home savings and loan association. Second and third mortgages carry higher interest rates—often beginning at 8 or 10 per cent depending on the area, state laws, and availability of money. Savings and loan associations are also profitable where first-mortgage interest rates are high (6 per cent or more).

MORTGAGES CAN EXPAND YOUR CAPITAL

Nearly $20 billion per year is available for real estate mortgages. You can obtain some of this money to finance your way to a spare-time second-income fortune. Wise use of mortgages can give you 100 per cent financing of some projects. In others, you might combine a commercial loan with a mortgage for 100 per cent financing. Three mortgage techniques you should know are refinancing, multiple mortgages, and commercial loans combined with mortgages. We'll take a quick look at each.

Refinancing can pay off. Let's say you own a rental building which is 30 years old. You bought it recently for $35,000, paying $4,000 down and financing the balance with a $31,000 mortgage. You would like to renovate the building by spending about $10,000 to modernize the bathrooms, wiring, lighting fixtures, refrigerators, and entrance hallway. When the modernization is complete you believe the new valuation of the building will be $50,000, based on the higher rents that can be charged, But since most lending agencies make a counter offer of a smaller loan when you try to refinance a mortgage, you decide to raise the new valuation to $53,000.

Prepare income and expense statements for the building based on the *new valuation.* Chapter 9 shows a typical form. Have your statement neatly typed, in triplicate. Make an appointment with the mortgage loan officer in your bank and be on time. Describe your modernization plan briefly. Leave two copies of the statement with the loan officer, after answering any questions he asks. Tell him to call you when the loan has been approved or rejected. You will be asked to prepare a financial statement during the interview. Give accurate information in the statement. Be certain that you fill out the form as neatly as possible.

Within a week you should have an answer from the bank. Let's assume the loan is approved for $50,000. What does this mean to you? You will receive $50,000. With this you pay off the existing $31,000 mortgage, leaving $19,000. From the $19,000 you must deduct the $10,000 for modernization, leaving $9,000 in cash. If you deduct your $4,000 down payment on the building you still have $5,000 cash left over. With this cash you might purchase another building and modernize it. Thus, you have recovered your original investment and cash to spare for a new venture.

In a variation of refinancing you can use your own home as a source of cash. If you've made mortgage payments for three years or more you can probably obtain $1,000, or much more, depending on the amount of the original mortgage, its duration (15, 20, 25, or 30 years), and the interest rate. This is sometimes called "buying your own home." In a recent year more than $10 billion was obtained by home owners who refinanced their homes.

Let's say you bought your home 10 years ago with a 20-year mortgage for $17,000 at 6 per cent interest. By refinancing now you would obtain approximately $6,050 cash. From this you would deduct about $550 for closing costs, title search, legal fees, and others, leaving about $5,500. Such a sum would be an excellent base from which to start your second-income spare-time business. This example assumes you refinance for the same amount as in the original mortgage. Should your home appreciate in value you might be able to refinance for more, giving you a larger amount of cash.

When considering refinancing keep these facts in mind: (1) Try to obtain your loan from the present holder of your mortgage—he may be able to restore the existing mortgage to its original amount, saving you closing costs, title-search and other fees. (2) If you are turned down by one lender, try another. Some lenders may be short of cash while others have surplus cash and are anxious for your business. Be sure to check with savings banks, commercial banks, home savings and loan associations, insurance companies, and private mortgage brokers. (3) Follow the hints given earlier in this chapter when filling out the loan form. (4) Try to obtain the lowest interest rate possible on the new mortgage. However, if your original loan was at 4¾ per cent don't expect to obtain this rate today. Like almost everything else, mortgage costs have risen. (5) You will usually have 30 days in which to accept the loan after your application is approved, so if you're not completely satisfied with the terms, shop around immediately.

(6) When contemplating purchase of rental property which you will modernize, try to obtain an indication from a mortgage lender as to how large a loan you could obtain based on the new valuation. To do this, prepare an income and expense statement. The reaction of lenders to your application can quickly indicate if the venture is worth your time. (7) Always be sure to check for loan fees or bonuses *before* signing the mortgage papers. Some brokers charge 1 to 2 per cent to arrange a mortgage; others require a flat-fee bonus. Try not to get into a financial position where you have to pay high fees or bonuses—your profits will be reduced.

(8) Try to obtain an open-end provision in every new mortgage. This provision allows you to borrow the amount paid off on a mortgage without having a new mortgage written. Many new mortgages, and some older ones, contain this provision. Check your existing mortgage to see if it has an open-end provision before you begin to shop for a new mortgage.

MULTIPLE MORTGAGES

Also called subsidiary mortgages, or secondary financing, multiple mortgages are widely used for income properties like apartment houses, motels, rooming houses, and hotels. Probably the second mortgage is the most common. But some properties carry as many as seven mortgages. In your spare-time second-income fortune building you would be wise to limit the number of mortgages on any property to three. Beyond this you can get so involved that your profits are wasted.

Second and third mortgages carry high interest rates because the lender's risks are greater. You'll also have to pay higher fees or bonuses to the lender or broker. Here are a few ideas to keep in mind about multiple mortgages:

1. An anxious seller may be willing to take a second mortgage on a property so that the bank mortgage, plus the second mortgage, gives you control of the property with no down payment. Keep this in mind, for even if he won't take a second mortgage for the full down payment he may be willing to finance a portion of it. This reduces the amount of cash you must invest.

2. Don't be discouraged by high interest rates, fees, or bonuses on second and third mortgages. If multiple mortgages give you control of profitable property, pay the cost and be glad you are making a profit. Some day you will be in a position to lend. Then you'll collect high interest, fees, or bonuses.

3. Use mortgages flexibly. Thus, a second or third mortgage might be used to pay a real estate agent's fee. This saves you some cash, and you pay only nominal interest costs.

4. Pay off second and third mortgages as soon as possible out of the earnings of the property. You will then be in a better position to sell the property, or to take out another mortgage to obtain more cash.

COMMERCIAL LOANS COMBINED WITH MORTGAGES

Suppose you are interested in buying an income property for $27,000. The required down payment is $5,000 and the owner refuses to take a second mortgage for this or any other amount. What might you do?

Obtain a *renewable* six-month commercial loan for $5,000. Follow all the hints given earlier when applying for the loan. Pay the interest on the loan *every* month. Each month, save as much income from the property as possible. On the *fifth* month pay the interest, plus as much of the principal as possible. Why the fifth month? Because the following month, when you want to renew, the bank will be much more willing to do so since you have shown your desire to pay off the loan in advance.

Continue making monthly interest payments, with a payment on the principal every fifth month. Renew the loan every six months.

Using commercial loans this way you can obtain your income property with no money down. Of course, you could use the money for improvements, repairs, or other purposes that will increase your operating profits.

KNOW THE COST OF BORROWED CAPITAL

You *can* finance your way to a second-income spare-time fortune. But it costs money to borrow money. Some people speak of this cost as the "rent" they pay to use a certain sum of money for a specific time. Bankers call this rent by another name—interest. You can keep financing costs low in three ways: (1) Use as little capital as possible. (2) Use commercial loans whenever they are available to you. (3) Know the cost of borrowed capital.

We discussed the first two items earlier in this chapter. Now we'll turn our attention to the price you'll have to pay for borrowed capital.

Some people have hazy ideas about interest rates. They are confused by the various terms used when talking about loans. Since you are interested in building a spare-time second-income fortune, you probably know more about interest rates than most people. But you are also interested in broadening your knowledge of finance. The following paragraphs show you the smart-money approach to analyzing the cost of your borrowed capital.

True interest is the rate you pay based on the *average* amount of money available to you from a loan. Let's say you borrowed $1,000 for one year at an interest rate of 5 per cent. You will have to pay back $1,000 + 0.05 ($1,000) = $1,050. The payment on this loan would be $87.50 per month for twelve months. In the first six months you would pay back 6(87.50) = $525, or half of $1,050. Thus, for the next six months you have only $525 available from the $1,000 you received. If you were to compute the *average* amount of money available to you throughout the year from this $1,000 loan it would be $500. Since you are paying $50 (= 0.05 × $1,000) for the use of $500 for one year the *true interest rate* is $50/$500 = 0.10, or 10 per cent. This shows you that the stated interest rate is actually half the true interest rate.

Why use true interest rate? Because it is the simplest measure you can use to compare the cost of two or more loans. Also, you can compute a true interest rate using only arithmetic. With a little experience you can mentally figure true interest rate. This is a useful skill when you are trying to size up a deal or loan quickly.

Banks, finance companies, and money brokers use many different terms to describe interest costs. Thus, you'll read of a charge of "1 per cent per month on the unpaid balance." This is often called *monthly interest.* Multiply the monthly rate by twelve to obtain the true interest rate. Since an interval of one year is always used in figuring your interest rate, the *true annual interest rate* for the above loan is twelve months (0.01) = 0.12, or 12 per cent. Some small loan companies charge as high as 42 per cent true annual interest rates on their loans.

Many banks make personal loans at a rate of 4 per cent *discounted*— that is, deducted in advance from the amount you borrow. Let's say you borrow $1,000 for a year at 4 per cent discount. You receive $960 (= $1,000 − 0.04 $\times$ 1000). Your monthly payment would be $80. The average amount of money you would have during the year from this loan is $960/2 = $480. Thus, the true annual interest rate is $40/$480 = 0.0833, or 8.33 per cent.

Some banks charge *add-on* interest. To do this they add the interest charge to the amount you borrow and divide by twelve to obtain the monthly payment. Let's say you borrow $1,000 at 5 per cent add-on interest. Thus, you must pay back $1,000 + 0.05 (1000) = $1,050. The average amount of money you have is $500 and the interest charge is $50. Therefore, the true annual interest rate is $50/$500 = 0.10, or 10 per cent.

As these two examples show, all you need do to find the approximate true annual interest rate on discounted and add-on loans is double the stated interest rate.

Many finance companies never state the interest rate charged. Instead, a "carrying charge" is given. For instance, if you borrow $3,600 and the carrying charge for three years is $900, the *average* amount of money you'll have from this loan is $3,600/3 = $1,200; and the *annual* interest charge is $900/3 = $300. Your true annual interest rate is therefore $300/$1200 = 0.25, or 25 per cent.

On some loans you will have multiple rates—as 2 per cent per month on the first $3,000; 1 per cent per month on the next $1,000, and so on. To obtain the approximate true annual interest rate on these loans, multiply the maximum stated rate by twelve. Thus, the approximate true annual rate on this loan would be 2(12) = 24 per cent. This is a trifle higher than the actual rate, but accurate enough for most business purposes.

There are banks, finance companies, and loan brokers who will charge you certain fees for your loan. These fees are given various names —investigation costs, credit-checking, bonus, finder's fee, or life insurance. How should you treat these when computing true annual interest? There is only one way—add all these costs to the interest charge, if the loan is for one year. Where the loan is for more than one year, divide the sum of these costs and the total interest by the number of years the loan is to run. Divide the result by the amount borrowed to find the true annual interest rate.

SUCCESSFUL SPARE-TIME BUSINESS FINANCING: A SUMMARY

You CAN finance your way to a second-income spare-time fortune. Good financing is a must if you want to build a major fortune. Keep the following points in mind. (1) Get by with little capital. (2) Seek low-capital projects. (3) Make maximum use of low-cost bank financing. (4) Consider private and public stock offerings. (5) Use a factor to increase your cash on hand. (6) Generate cash with a sale and leaseback. (7) Sell before you buy to improve your cash position. (8) Don't overlook the cash potential of the SBIC. (9) Explore ALL capital sources. (10) Try smart-money capital-raising methods. (11) Expand your capital with good mortgages. (12) Combine commercial loans with mortgages. (13) Know the cost of borrowed capital.

6	You don't have to wait until tomorrow to begin building your second-income spare-time fortune. Today—at this very moment —is the time to begin. You don't need thousands of dollars in capital, a place of business, telephone, or any equipment. All you need is the desire for a larger income and a determination to obtain it. So let's take the next step towards your spare-time second-income fortune.

Fortunes are built from the ideas of men and women. You can spend years longing for money, but until you have **a** |

Start Building

Your Second-Income

Fortune Today

good idea, real money won't be yours. So your first step, after resolving to build a second-income spare-time fortune, is to develop your idea sources. It's easy to do this when you know how. Start now to use the following ten money-laden idea sources.

1. *Regularly read a good business newspaper.* The *Wall Street Journal* is excellent. *Barron's, The Journal of Commerce,* and others, are also helpful. For the first few months read every item in your business newspaper. You'll learn much about business procedures, opportunities, financing, and laws. Study the advertisements. The Business Opportunities, Capital to Invest, Capital Wanted, and Real Estate classified advertisements can be highly useful. These sections of the paper will keep you up to date on the newest developments in business. Make notes on every idea you get from the paper. Clip ads and file them for future use.

A good friend of mine, Michael F., became enthused about building a second-income spare-time fortune after I spent some time showing him the advantages of extra dollars. Michael had one weakness—he loved to sail a boat. The only trouble was that he couldn't afford to support his wife, three children, *and* a sailboat. For several months I urged him to become a regular reader of a business newspaper. After some argument, he agreed to do so.

Three weeks later he called me. Excitedly, he told me about an ad in the Business Opportunities column of his business newspaper. A sailboat manufacturer, looking for people to demonstrate his boats, offered a 60 per cent discount on a new boat, and hefty commissions on every boat sold after a demonstration. Further, the manufacturer would lend chosen salesmen the price of a demonstration boat. My friend wired the manufacturer and soon had his sailboat. That summer, while enjoying his sailing hobby with his family, he sold fifteen sailboats. His commissions far exceeded the cost of his boat. Today he continues to sail and sell— all the result of one three-line ad that gave him an idea.

Scan the business section of your daily and Sunday newspaper for useful fortune-building ideas. Many excellent papers such as *The New York Times, Los Angeles Times, Louisville Courier Journal,* and others are fine sources of business ideas. Some of these papers run short biographies of business leaders. Read these stories; they are full of useful ideas you can apply to your own life. Marvin Glass, said to be the world's most successful toy designer (Mister Machine, Odd Ogg, Kissy Doll, Robot

Commando, King Zov, and many others), reads widely. He keeps his creativity active by regular reading of the *Wall Street Journal, Scientific American*, the *New Republic, Punch*, and many books. He is also a careful observer of people and their lives.

2. *Read at least one business magazine a week.* There are many excellent business magazines—*Business Week, Fortune, Forbes, Dun's Review and Modern Industry*—that present a deep coverage of business news and give much background information you can use.

Several years ago *Business Week* published a number of articles on Regulation A stock offerings. These articles gave me the idea to offer the stock of one of my companies to the public. Since the articles discussed many of the procedures to follow, I found it easy to prepare the offering.

Fortune's series of articles on "Personal Investing" give many useful ideas on making profits in stocks, bonds, mutual funds, commodities, and lesser known issues. *Business Week's* "Market Briefs" present excellent coverage of the stock market. One of my professional colleagues read a short item in one magazine about speculators using "no-load" mutual funds as a source of profits during a rising stock market. Since "no-load" means the fund operates without sales or redemption fees, a speculator can buy and sell fund shares free of charge. This short item gave my colleague a money-making idea. Being a speculator, he immediately bought no-load mutual funds because the market was on the rise. Shortly before the market topped out he sold—at a profit.

Take out a subscription to a business magazine, or go to your local library. Most town and city libraries have copies of the leading business magazines you can read free of charge. Make notes of any ideas you obtain from the magazines on three by five inch file cards. Carry the cards with you wherever you go so you can add ideas that occur to you during the day.

3. *Read several trade magazines in your fields of interest.* Trade magazines present the technical side of your business interests. Thus, if you're thinking of selling farming equipment in your spare time (an excellent way to earn good commissions on no investment other than time), read *Agricultural Equipment Dealer, Farm and Power Equipment*, and *Farm Power*. Each of these is an excellent source of good ideas and helpful information. Regular reading of these and similar magazines for a year or more will broaden your knowledge more than you think possible.

There are thousands of fine trade magazines devoted to subjects ranging from accident prevention to yachting. Each is full of money-making ideas you can use. What's more, your new knowledge will give you a greater zest for life, making you happier and more productive. To obtain a comprehensive list of trade magazines, study a copy of Standard Rate and Data Service, Inc., *Business Publication Rates and Data,* available in large libraries.

Another excellent source of ideas is the *house magazine.* These magazines are published by companies, banks, associations, and other organizations to promote their ideas and interests. About 7,000 different house magazines are published in the United States today. Most are distributed free of charge to people requesting them. Subjects range from advertising to zip-feed mills. For a comprehensive guide to more than 4,000 leading house magazines consult the *Gebbie Press House Magazine Directory* in your local library.

4. *Try to read six inspirational and self-improvement books each year.* There are many excellent books of this type on the market today. Here are six I found very helpful. I'm sure you'll enjoy them too:

J. D. Cooper, *How to Get More Done in Less Time,* Doubleday, 1962

W. E. Edwards, *10 Days to a Great New Life,* Prentice-Hall, 1963

Bernard Haldane, *How to Make a Habit of Success,* Prentice-Hall, 1960

Vernon Howard, *Time Power for Personal Success,* Prentice-Hall, 1960

D. I. Rogers, *Make Your Income Count,* Henry Holt, 1958

D. A. Laird, *The Technique of Getting Things Done,* McGraw-Hill, 1947

Inspirational books like these, as well as the one you are now reading, can build your enthusiasm and drive. They will also provide many useful ideas which can help you build your fortune. Never underestimate the power of an inspirational book; it can give you the incentive to build a fortune during the 2,000 spare-time hours available to you every year.

5. *Read good books on the business that interests you.* There are thousands of fine books on good business practices in all sorts of money-making activities. You will find many listed in the *Subject Guide to Books*

in Print, available in almost every public library. A recent issue listed some 100,000 books under 24,000 headings with 30,000 cross references.

Buy copies of at least two books on the business that interests you. By reading the books of two or more authors you obtain a broader knowledge of your subject. Topics you do not understand in one book may be clearer in the other. Whenever you increase your knowledge of a business your creativity and enthusiasm expand. Ideas flow to you more readily, improving your chances for outstanding success.

Twelve talented commercial artists, including Albert Dorne and Norman Rockwell, had an idea for a new kind of correspondence school. They founded Famous Artists Schools, Inc., in an old mill in Westport, Conn. Fifteen years later every $50 these artists invested to found the school was worth $27,000—and still growing. These highly successful men knew their business; they spent many hours perfecting their skills.

You, too, can perfect your skills, if you make the effort to learn as much as possible about the business that interests you. Reading good books about your spare-time business is an excellent way to build your skills. So start today—business books will provide the technical facts you need; inspirational books will keep your enthusiasm and interest high. As William Feather, publisher, author, and business philosopher wrote, "Whatever your job is, there are books whose subjects cover your work. I advise every normal person to seek such books, buy them, and read them. Why spend five years gaining experience when, by the purchase of a book, you can learn what the experience of others has been?"

6. *Talk to people in business.* Get to know profit potentials of various businesses; operating costs; risks you must take; problems you will face. By talking with businessmen you will obtain firsthand facts to guide you in your second-income spare-time fortune hunt. One idea gleaned this way can put you on the road to a big income.

Talking to businessmen has many advantages. You will quickly learn if a particular business would be satisfying to you. Problems—and every business has them—will be made crystal clear to you. By observing a man's clothing, automobile, and way of life while you talk to him, you will be able to learn if his business should be your business.

While talking to a businessman try to learn: (a) how and when he started, (b) how and where he obtained his original financing, (c) what his normal profit ratio is, (d) what his major problems are and how he solves them, and (e) what sort of future he sees for his business. Other questions will occur while you talk. Keep one fact in mind at all times when in the company of successful businessmen: You learn when you listen. If you fill the conversation with your ideas you'll have little chance to learn. So close your mouth—*and listen*. You'll be amazed at how much you can learn this way.

7. *Listen to businessmen at idle moments.* You'll often overhear businessmen talking—in a restaurant, on a plane or train. These conversations can be full of ideas for you. I'm not recommending that you purposely eavesdrop, but if a conversation is so loud you can't avoid hearing it, then listen.

I've overheard many such conversations on planes and commuting trains. Probably the greatest benefit I derived from the conversations was a better understanding of businessmen. I've also gleaned many interesting business facts, giving me a better understanding of my own problems and ways to solve them. So listen and learn.

8. *Observe general business procedures and conditions.* Open your eyes and see the business around you. The next time you go into a store, take a good look at the stock, the number of customers, how much each purchases, and the store itself. Do the same when you're on a plane, in a school, a doctor's or dentist's office.

Try to estimate the average expenditure of each person. Translate this into the number of customers or clients per day, week, month, year. Simple multiplication will give you the annual gross business.

"It's only a guess," you say. Of course—and it's probably a wrong guess. But as your experience grows, your guesses will be more accurate. Then you'll dignify them with a different name—estimates. The more estimates you make, the better equipped you'll be to size up a business that interests you.

Make "dry-run" estimates of business situations you observe. Buy a good introductory book on accounting procedures. J. K. Lasser's *Accounting for Everyday Profit*, American Research Council, is an excellent little volume. Apply the procedures you learn to estimate costs, profits, taxes, and other factors. Try to find the hourly return of each business you observe. The facts you glean will expand your know-how and grasp of business potentials.

9. *Make full use of trade-association data.* There are more than 12,000 national and local trade associations in the United States. Two helpful publications of the U.S. Department of Commerce which give data on a variety of associations are *National Associations of the United States* and *Directory of National Trade Associations.* Both are available at larger public libraries.

What is a trade association? The U.S. Department of Commerce gives this definition in the second book listed above: ". . . a nonprofit, cooperative, organization of business competitors designed to assist its members and its industry in dealing with mutual business problems in such areas as accounting practices, business ethics, commercial and industrial research, standardization, statistics, trade promotion, relations with government employees, and the general public."

What can a trade association do for you in your search for a second-income fortune? Plenty. An alert association can provide valuable statistics on profits, costs, number of employees needed, correct trade practices, actual and potential competition, advertising procedures, sales promotion techniques, market surveys and analyses, commercial standards, and so on. You can often glean more useful information in a few hours at a trade association than you can by any other means. Of course, books and actual observation will round out your background knowledge.

So make full use of trade-association data. Never be embarrassed about writing, calling, or visiting a trade association to ask for information. Most trade association officials are willing, friendly, and helpful. They will expend much time and effort to provide the data you need about their industry.

10. *Keep up to date on business conditions.* Read the financial pages of your daily and Sunday papers. Keep track of the state of business. Unless you know what's going on in the world of business you have little chance of success. Rolf Millqvist, founder and owner of a large discount store in Stockholm, Sweden, knew the exact condition of business when he opened his first small store. For three years he operated the store as its silent owner while holding the position of financial director of a large food packer and processor. Sales rose 100 times in 10 years, rising from $50,000 the first year to $5 million in the tenth year. Its list of regular customers grew from less than 100 to 20,000.

Of course, Rolf Millqvist knew more than the condition of business.

He also had an *idea*—one that was to pay off. His first idea was to start an American-style supermarket. He gave this idea up when he realized that a successful supermarket depended on the customers driving to it. Then he thought, "Why can't the shop drive to the customers?" Cars were scarce in Sweden, but nearly every home had a telephone. So Rolf founded a telephone-order discount store that delivers goods to the customer's home by truck. Today his business continues to grow even though Sweden has the second largest auto population in Europe. His success shows what a man can achieve with a spare-time beginning, if he is alert to good ideas and knows what's going on in the business world.

INVESTIGATE PROFITABLE SECOND-INCOME IDEAS

Never let a good idea die—do something about it. Every time you allow a good idea to wither something will "die" in you. We all know people who are constantly getting "brilliant" ideas. But these ideas always seem to fade away. Nothing comes of them. Should you ask them about a discarded idea you'll receive a lame excuse. Time passes and the people with the brilliant ideas gradually lose their appeal. Soon these people are regarded as failures, dreamers who never did much.

Why do such people fail? There is only one reason—they didn't put their ideas into action. They toyed with ideas, dropping one after another without investigation. Don't let this happen to you. Your second-income fortune will never be more than a rosy dream unless you investigate each profitable idea you get. Here are three positive steps you can take to size up good money-making ideas.

1. *Develop a numbers-sense for projects that interest you.* As you saw earlier in this chapter, you can make "dry-run" estimates of the potential of a business. To develop a numbers-sense for business, analyze many potential projects. Do this by obtaining data about businesses that interest you from business brokers, ads in newspapers, and people who want to sell their business. Study each project to obtain a clear idea of costs, profits, and the time you must devote to the business.

Compare large and small businesses. A friend of mine, Dan T., decided to open a spare-time trucking business to build a second income. Dan immediately faced a difficult problem: How many trucks did he need to achieve his wealth goal (Chapter 3) of $1,000 per month spare-time income? I advised Dan to study twenty trucking concerns, ranging from one-man one-truck firms to those having a fleet of several hundred trucks.

Dan spent several months studying the profit-and-loss statements of twenty firms. These statements revealed many useful facts such as the cost of insurance, truck depreciation allowances, gasoline costs, maintenance costs, labor charges, and other important information. By the time three months had passed, Dan knew exactly how long a good truck would last, how many miles he could get from a set of tires, and the average profit per mile of truck operation. To organize his data in a useful manner Dan set up a file for each company. After some further study of several good business books on the trucking industry, and the best trade journals in the field, Dan bought three trucks—the number his studies showed would be most profitable to him. Today Dan's spare-time business is booming and he is achieving his second-income fortune goal.

Dan was successful for several reasons. He developed a numbers-sense for the business he found interesting. He obtained complete information on every project he thought profitable. He set up a data file on each project, even though he knew he might not invest in some of them. Finally, he researched his spare-time business by reading good books, trade journals, and newspapers.

2. *Go where the business is.* Don't confine your research to profit-and-loss statements, books, and magazines. Get out and go where the business is. If you're thinking of spare-time ownership of a service station —a profitable sideline for many fortune builders—visit as many local service stations as you can. Earlier you learned how to observe *general* business conditions. With the experience gained there you will be better qualified to observe *specific* conditions. Make complete notes on what you observe. Keep an accurate file of these notes.

Paul A., a successful engineer with a large electronics company, operated a string of fifteen profitable service stations in his spare time. He used the profits from one station to buy another. When a friend of his wanted to open an engineering research firm, Paul sold several of his service stations and used the profits to found the research firm, with his friend as president. Today Paul's spare-time income exceeds his full-time job income, but he keeps his job because he likes the stimulating ideas he gets from working in the fast-moving electronics field.

Go where the business is. See the business at all seasons of the year.

Each season brings different problems to every business. Heavy snowfalls can reduce your income by restricting customer travel and raising your labor bill if extra help is needed for snow clearing. Excessive heat in summer can lead to water shortages, long operation of cooling equipment, and possible motor burnout. So try to see your future business *before* you buy it the way you'd see it *after* you buy it. Put yourself in the owner's place. You may decide that what appears to be a profitable business would be unappealing to your temperament.

Learn why a business is for sale. Don't accept the usual reasons—age, illness, retirement,—until after you've made a thorough study of the business. If you are thinking of starting a new business, try to determine why someone else hasn't done so. Seek out the possible trouble spots in any business—faulty equipment, excessive labor rates, or cranky customers. One undesirable condition can ruin the profit potentials of a business, *unless* your past experience is such that you know how to overcome the problem. Remember this about any spare-time second-income business: the fewer problems the business has the easier it will be for you to operate. Locate a problem-free, low-profit business rather than a problem-ridden, high-profit business. It's usually easy to raise the profits of a problem-free business because you can concentrate on income without worrying about other problems.

3. *Analyze your findings.* Study your notes. Rid yourself of bias—don't let your personal interest in a subject sway your business judgment. Several years ago I was almost trapped by personal interest. As a youth I sailed in the U.S. Merchant Marine. Ever since then I've loved ships and shipping. One of my books earned an extra large royalty and I decided to invest the money in the stock of several steamship lines. As I studied the stocks of these lines I was appalled by the low earnings and dismal future prospects.

I asked myself, "Why do I buy stock?" The answer was clear: "To earn a profit." But steamship stocks, at that time, were highly unprofitable. Then why did I want them? For a purely personal reason—because I thought it would be nice to own a "piece" of a steamship line. Thus, a personal interest almost led me to make a poor business decision.

So start building your second-income fortune today by analyzing the data you collected. *Use* your data to compute probable costs, profits and losses. When figuring costs, try to estimate the time you'll spend running your spare-time business. Along with the time, try to find how much aggravation you'll meet.

I always try to predict what I call the "aggravation factor" in a business because I'm the type of guy who enjoys being left alone. The aggravation aspect of a business was made clear to me during my first venture in spare-time operation of rental real estate. I owned a one-family house which was easy to keep profitably rented. The first rental was to a family having several children. Shortly after the family moved in I began receiving nightly phone calls. "Johnnie kicked out the front-door screen." "Suzie broke a window." After four such calls I was ready to sell the house. I mulled it over and decided to try to put someone between myself and the tenant. An agent was the answer. For a nominal fee I hired an agent and he took all the complaints from then on.

If you enjoy talking to people, choose a business involving personal contact. But if you prefer to have an uninterrupted family life, then pick a mail-order business, or an activity in which you can be one step removed from the customer.

Once you've analyzed your findings, take action. Make a decision—and start building your second-income fortune in your spare time.

TAKE POSITIVE ACTION ON GOOD IDEAS

Don't allow inaction or fear of making decisions to slow you in your quest for spare-time wealth. To successfully build your second-income fortune you must overcome indecision and eliminate fear.

Money flows to the decision-maker; it seems to avoid the weak, the indecisive. Why be afraid to make a decision? Nothing begins or ends until you make a decision. What if you make a wrong decison? You must correct it. But remember this: *once you make a decision, even a wrong one, you are on the way to your second-income fortune. Wrong decisions can be corrected; decisions that are never made lead only to disappointment.* Resolve today that you will make decisions sooner, faster, more confidently. Here are five hints to help you make profitable second-income decisions.

1. *Don't delay—act now.* Your decision may be yes or no. Regardless of what it is, *act now*—after you have studied the facts. Don't say "I'll decide next week." Too many interruptions may occur between

now and next week. Study your facts, analyze your data, make your decision—take action.

2. *Profit from the advantages of taking action.* Build your enthusiasm. Get moving. Begin making the money flow in. Nothing succeeds like success. Taking action can build your income; sitting tight keeps your mind and dollars inactive. Action brings rewards; inaction dulls your enthusiasm.

3. *Check your progress—make any needed corrections.* You can't correct an action until after you've begun to take it. So, whenever you make a decision related to your part-time second income, watch closely for results. Compare your costs and profits with the estimates you made earlier. If costs begin to exceed the estimates, find out why. Make a decision to do something about excessive costs; then take action.

It is the rare person who makes a correct decision in every situation, so don't be afraid to alter your thinking when you see that it is necessary. Get into the habit of constantly comparing your results with your objectives. Remember that results pay off—higher profits will put you nearer the fortune you desire.

4. *Don't look back—push ahead.* Looking back only shows you where you've been. Looking ahead shows you where you might go. William Stern, a director of Northwest Airlines, didn't look behind but kept pushing forward. This attitude has made him an officer in three real estate concerns and a clothing store. He was also president of the Dakota National Bank. Besides his many business interests, Bill Stern found time for politics and became a National Committeeman for one of the two major political parties in the United States.

Actions mean results. Forward-moving actions bring you nearer the profits that will build your second-income fortune. So push ahead—build your future by moving towards it today.

5. *Use actions to prove your decisions.* The more correct decisions you make, the greater your self-confidence. Direct all your energies and actions to prove your decisions. Not only will you show that your decision was correct, but you'll also obtain the results you desire. Make decisions and actions an integral part of your fortune search and you'll move ahead faster and more surely. Make your first big decision now—that you will start building your second-income fortune today.

Numbers are always a part of building a second-income fortune in your spare time. You can't get away from numbers—they keep popping up whenever you think, plan, or take action in business. To be successful you must begin now to play the numbers game of wealth.

7

The numbers game of a second-income fortune begins with the capital you need to start your business. Many beginners assume that they need several thousand dollars to begin a spare-time business. Forget that right now. If you develop a good

Play the Numbers

Game of Wealth

numbers sense you will soon reject every business idea requiring more capital than you have. You'll seek, instead, those projects you can manage with the money you have.

One fortune builder, an engineer, began tinkering in his basement with specialized industrial measuring and detecting instruments. From this smart start his firm developed into a thriving electronics manufacturer. In nine years another man went from a $25-a-week rancher and ski instructor to head of his own insurance company. When he needed capital to found his firm, this man personally raised more than $1 million by selling 3,000 shares of stock at $350 per share. His total sales expense was less than $30,000. William Morris, founder of the British Motor Corporation, began building bicycles at the age of 16. His starting capital: $11.60. During his career he gave away $116 million, chiefly for medical and scientific research.

Each of these talented and resourceful fortune builders knew, or quickly learned, the numbers aspect of wealth when he began. You, too, must develop a good numbers sense if you expect to become wealthy. Let's take a quick look at how you can play the numbers game of wealth while building your second-income fortune.

1. *Capital needs.* Don't let a number frighten you. *Try to see how to reduce it to smaller, more manageable numbers.* The man above did just this when faced with the need for $1 million to found his insurance company. Instead of trying to sell one share of stock for $1 million he sold 3,000 shares at $350 each. It certainly is easier to sell a share for $350 than it is for $1 million.

You need only $1,000? $10,000? Use the same approach. Ten $100 loans from friends will give you $1,000; one hundred $100 loans will give you $10,000. No matter how large or small a sum you need to start a business, breaking it into smaller amounts makes your task easier.

Some years ago while trying to raise $5,000 for a business venture I became very discouraged. My family was young; we had just moved into a new house; my new car sat in the driveway. Where could I get $5,000 in a hurry? At the time I was writing articles for trade magazines in my spare time. The payment for an article usually ranged between $50 and $100. One night, while thinking about the $5,000 I needed I asked myself, "How many '$50-articles' can I write in a month?" I checked my records and found that I could probably average ten "$50-articles" per month. Thus, in about ten months I would have the $5,000 I needed.

What had I done? I had played the numbers game of wealth. As long as I thought of $5,000 my mind was a blank—the sum was too large to face with confidence. But once I reduced it to *smaller, more manageable numbers* I lost my fright. Also, I unknowingly applied a second valuable principle: *Think in terms of sums which you can easily obtain.* In my case it was "$50-articles." Incidentally, my average income exceeded $50 per article and I accumulated the $5,000 in about seven months.

There are many other numbers related to your capital needs. In Chapter 5 we discussed some of these—true and apparent interest rates, loan payoff time, refinancing, etc. Buy a good book on business arithmetic and review the many shortcuts you can use to compute interest costs, installment payments, note and draft discounts, mortgage and down payments. Wise use of arithmetic shortcuts will enable you to make quick estimates during business conferences and discussions. This skill will bring you many benefits while you are building your second-income fortune. An excellent book which I find very helpful is: R. R. Rosenberg and Harry Lewis, *Essentials of Business Arithmetic*, McGraw-Hill, 1964.

2. *Figuring your profits.* Once you invest some time and money in a spare-time business you'll want to figure your profits; for profits, you know, are the key numbers in fortune building.

Profit, which can be expressed in dollars or per cent, is the difference between your sales price and your total cost for the item or service. This simple definition can be applied to any spare-time business you may operate—from the manufacture of a product to rendering a personal service like teaching or consulting.

What dollar amounts and profit percentages will you seek? You'll want the largest dollar profits you can achieve, perhaps $5,000 during your first year in a part-time business. Aim at a high net operating profit. That is the profit after all *direct* and *indirect* costs have been deducted from the total income. *Direct costs* are those you can charge directly to a product or service you sell. Thus, the cost of lumber for a cabinet you build and offer for sale is a direct cost. But the cost of the grease to lubricate the power saw you use to build a number of cabinets is an *indirect cost,* because it is almost impossible to find how much grease is used by the saw while you are building one cabinet.

In all my part-time activities, I aim at a high net operating profit percentage—at least 30 per cent *before* taxes. You should aim at this or a higher percentage. If you aim lower, you may find that the time and effort you expend are very large in relation to the profit you obtain. So play the numbers game of profits—seek large dollar and high percentage profits.

Get to know the numbers of retail sales, if they are involved in your spare-time business. Refer to your business arithmetic book for a review on how to find the net price with a given trade discount, use of a discount series (two or more discounts), finding the single discount equivalent to a discount series, cash-discounts figuring and net cash price, markups and per cent markup, retail sales price and its relation to cost and markup, the breakeven point, and other relevant procedures. Learn how to use discount and markup tables. Quick figuring of retail sales profits enables you to bargain with ease.

When your spare-time business is a "money business," (see Chapter 5) you'll have to know the *present worth* of the income you'll be receiving from people who borrow money from you. This is easy to figure if you use the compound-interest formula given in your business arithmetic book. There are several other key formulas related to interest and the time value of money that you'll want to learn. These cover simple interest, compound interest, present worth, uniform-series payments, sinking-fund deposits, capital recovery, and the present value of a uniform series. You'll find all these easy-to-use formulas in any good book on business arithmetic. Solve a number of problems using the formulas; you'll find them interesting and informative.

3. *Taxes are always important in building a second-income fortune in your spare time.* Recognize now that as your income increases, so will your taxes. Careful planning, along with a good knowledge of the legitimate tax deductions you can take, will permit you to keep your taxes at a low level. Once again you are faced with the numbers game of wealth. Chapter 13 gives many helpful tax suggestions for the spare-time wealth builder. Use these suggestions from the first day you go into business.

4. *Keep business differences in mind.* If you sell any item—a manufactured article, a piece of real estate, stocks, bonds,—you have certain costs you must pay. In the first place, you must pay for the article itself. This is the acquisition cost. Where you manufacture an article the acquisition cost may be the same as your manufacturing cost. With real estate, stocks,

or bonds, you have a purchase price which usually includes some kind of broker's fee. If you hold real estate for several months or longer before selling it you will probably have to pay property taxes. You may also have some maintenance fees. Stocks and bonds, being only slips of paper, require no maintenance and can be stored in a drawer or safe deposit box.

When you are ready to sell a product you must recover all your costs plus an additional amount if you are to show a profit. So, *know your costs*. One of the biggest causes of business failures is lack of knowledge of true costs in a business. To ensure an accurate knowledge of true costs, keep a careful record of every business expense you have. I do this in my various business activities by carrying a small expense and tax record book with me at all times. Every time I spend any money I make a record of it. Where the expense is business-connected, I obtain a receipt. At the end of the month I enter all my expenses in a large record book I keep at home.

Accurate record keeping has many advantages. It enables you to determine your *true* costs before you sell a product. With these true costs available it is easier for you to compute your actual profit. Your records will help you support the tax deductions you claim. Finally, the true costs and tax payments will help you answer accurately "Are my spare-time activities profitable?"

When you sell a service—like teaching, consulting, tax counseling, rental property—your costs may differ from those met in selling a product. Thus, in teaching and consulting, your expenses may be limited to travel, meals, lodgings, graphical display materials, and so forth. Rental property may require management fees, heating, painting. Or you may rent the property with the proviso that the tenant pay all these expenses. As with a product, however, you must know your true expenses—the numbers that mean the difference between a profit or a loss.

Recently a friend of mine had some money to invest. He was interested in purchasing one or more apartment houses. To obtain some idea of property values, offering prices, cash requirements, and return on investment he studied the real estate ads in one large city newspaper. This is a good approach, but provides only a limited view of the rental market. I suggested he check the "numbers" of rental property. Doing this he found the vacancy rate for all of New York City was 3.54 per cent, where rent control existed. Other nearby cities had lower vacancy rates—Chicago, 1.6; Cleveland, 1.7; Boston, 1.7; and Detroit, 1.8 percent—while rent controls were in effect. These numbers showed him that he should investigate several cities, instead of just one, if he wanted the highest and safest return on his investment. Once again, the numbers game of wealth proved out.

USE NUMBERS TO RELATE YOUR EFFORT TO YOUR FORTUNE

The saddest second-income fortune builders I know are those people who ignore the numbers and get on a profitless treadmill. They expend their time and energy for a break-even, or smaller, return. To them, their second-income fortune always seems to be just beyond their reach. These people ignore the four steps relating numbers to their effort and fortune. Here are these four powerful key steps. Use them now to ensure that your return is worth the effort you make.

1. *Convert your money goal into an effort goal.* Your dollar-per-hour beginning efforts are worthwhile if they build to $50 or $100 per hour. But if you work for years and your income never exceeds one dollar per hour, something is wrong.

Estimate, before you start a spare-time business, what your eventual hourly, weekly, monthly, or yearly income will be. At the same time, try to estimate how long it will take you to reach this income level. Then make a careful check of your income. If your desired income is not reached at about the time you forecast, find out why. Perhaps your time estimate was too optimistic; perhaps the business does not have the financial potential you thought it had.

Sell a nonprofitable or low-profit spare-time business as soon as you can after deciding the income is insufficient. But think twice before selling a profitable $30-per-hour business just because you estimated its potential as $50 per hour. Unless you are exceptionally talented, you are better off with a moderate spare-time income than with no income at all.

My experience while advising many spare-time fortune builders is that many of them underestimate the time required to build a fortune, and overestimate their potential financial return. Be ready for this tendency on your part until after you've gained some spare-time business experience.

Don't work for a tiny profit; your spare time is worth a hefty profit.

Convert your money goal into an effort goal of hours, weeks, months, years. Then work for your goal, carefully checking your progress at frequent intervals.

2. *Pace your efforts towards your fortune goal.* Work steadily. Don't worry about the speed at which you work; be more concerned about the quality of what you do. Among the spare-time fortune builders I advise are a number of beginning writers. These people are often surprised to learn that if they write 1,000 words per day (about four double-spaced typewritten pages) they can complete the typical 70,000-word non-fiction book or typical popular novel in less than three months. When they see a published book they never analyze its "numbers"—that is, the number of words, pages, and illustrations. If these beginning authors did analyze the numbers, and paced themselves to write about 1,000 words per day, they would soon be building a comfortable spare-time second-income fortune.

"Take time for all things," said Ben Franklin, one of America's greatest spare-time fortune builders. Don't try to rush into a second-income business because the money bug has bitten you. Take your time— "Too great haste leads us to error," wrote Moliere. Rushing into a business can lead to loss of your capital, delays, frustration. Take your time and find out what you want to do; then take the right steps.

Once your business is under way, work steadily. It is better to spend an hour an evening in steady, high-quality production than three hours in frantic, low-quality output. Use your head—think. Control your output so it is the best you can produce. Use your mind, your ingenuity, your creativity. P. D. Armour, the famous meat packer, said, "Anybody can cut prices, but it takes a brain to produce a better article." Pace your efforts to produce a better product or service, and your second-income fortune will build surely and steadily.

3. *Reassess your fortune goals at regular intervals.* Some second-income fortune builders earn quick, easy profits in their first spare-time business venture. They go on, year after year, earning a comfortable second income; but they never stop to ask, "Could I earn more?" Nor do they ask, "Could I earn the same income with less effort?"

To earn the maximum spare-time income you must stop every now and then to re-examine your fortune goals. I learned to do this after becoming an executive in a large, successful corporation.

Most corporations have at least two annual budgets—a *sales budget* and an *expense budget*. In the sales budget the probable sales for the coming year are predicted, month by month. The expense budget attempts to predict future operating costs in the same manner for the same period.

After several years of preparing budgets for my regular job I decided to apply this principle to my spare-time business activities. First I set up an expense budget, then an income budget. The results were spectacular. For the first time in my multi-activity life I had an over-all picture of my income and expenses. Today, I reassess my fortune goals at the end of every month. I compare budgeted (predicted) income with my actual income; budgeted (probable) expenses with actual expenses. This monthly reassessment of my fortune goals tells me exactly which activities are producing the best return. When I find that a certain business is failing to produce an adequate return, I sell it, if there is no hope of salvaging it.

Several second-income fortune builders to whom I recommended this procedure were horrified by the prospect of pages of budgets. Actually, you can keep all your budgets on one piece of standard size accounting paper, if you make entries neatly. These fortune-builders were easily convinced when I showed them my budgets. Today they, and hundreds of other second-income fortune builders, use this scheme to reassess their money goals every month.

Reassess your fortune goals at regular intervals and you will have positive command of your financial future. Neglect your income and you will find yourself on a treadmill leading to only mediocre profits.

4. *Alter your fortune goals when necessary.* Change is constant—existing sources of income fade and die. If you don't alter your fortune goals as conditions change you may find that your once-lucrative, spare-time second income is only a trickle of pennies. Frank W. Waskey, a man of many successful full- and spare-time businesses, went to Alaska in the gold-rush days of 1898. His first big strike came in 1905; two others came later. Between gold finds Waskey was elected a delegate to Congress. Later, he became the head of a mining concern, and director of a bank and a publishing company. He continued to prospect, roving by dogsled throughout Alaska. By the nineteen-forties, when the gold fever had subsided, Waskey was prospecting for other valuable minerals. In his mid-sixties he discovered a valuable cinnabar (ore of mercury)

mine. Thus, while other miners wasted their effort searching for nearly non-existent gold, Waskey altered his fortune goals and struck it big.

Don't think you are wedded forever to a spare-time business that returns you a good profit. If the market changes you may be left with little profit and big expenses. To avoid this, make a continuing study of the market for your product or service. When you detect a decrease in the market, consider the possibility of selling or trading your business. Get out while you are still making a profit. Invest the income from the sale in a new, more lucrative business. Pyramid your profits to raise your income.

Be flexible, alert, ready. Cast off the old when the new is more profitable. Alter your fortune goals when necessary. Don't allow sentiment to get in the way of profits. Unload the unprofitable, the declining, sick business. Stick with the robust, profitable, high-promise business.

THINK NUMBERS IF YOU WANT A SECOND-INCOME FORTUNE

Arithmetic frightened many of us in school. Don't let it scare you now. Beginning with this moment the arithmetic and numbers you deal with will be the figures of wealth—the wealth built from the positive success of your spare-time second-income fortune. Learn to think clearly and quickly; quick thinking pays off handsomely in the rough and aggressive world of the second-income fortune builder.

Make numbers a part of your daily life. Welcome a knowledge of costs, profits, markups, losses. Think profits; seek profits; build profits. Study business arithmetic, accounting, and finance. Learn now the time value of money. Apply numbers to every aspect of your spare-time business. You will prosper as you learn. Start a library of useful books which will quickly equip you to build a spare-time second-income with minimum effort. Buy the books from your local bookstore and begin studying now.

Most beginning second-income fortune builders have more time than money. So their real capital is time, not money. If you can turn time into money you can succeed in acquiring that all-important spare-time second-income fortune.

If you work five days a week you have about 2,000 hours per year of spare time available, assuming a two-week vacation. Certainly you cannot and will not work during every hour of your free time. But even if you work only 25 per cent of the time, or 500 hours, a fortune can be yours.

8

Make Time Work

for Your

Second-Income Fortune

Let's say you earn $10 per hour for 500 hours—your annual spare-time income will be $5,000. Raise your hourly income to $15 by using time more effectively and your income jumps to $7,500. And at $20 per hour you earn $10,000 per year spare-time income. Couldn't you use this much extra income every year of your life? Certainly you could. You can achieve it if you make maximum use of your spare time. For time is money—to you, to me, to every spare-time fortune builder. That's why you must learn to make time work for your second-income fortune.

Each spare-time dollar you earn is worth two dollars of your regular income. The extra income can be invested, saved, spent for a vacation, or used in many other ways. But most important of all—spare-time dollars can boost your fortune faster than any other earned income source.

Using your spare-time hours to build a fortune is one of the finest activities you'll ever undertake. Everyone, including yourself, benefits. Your family lives a better life on the dollars you bring in; you have more and wider interests and contacts; the product or service you sell benefits other people. Make your spare time your creative time and you will be more alive, more vibrant, more alert to yourself and the world around you.

BE MASTER OF YOUR FORTUNE-BUILDING TIME

Your spare time *can* be more productive. You can get more out of every spare-time hour if you use techniques similar to those popular with successful second-income fortune builders. Here are three powerful techniques you can use to quadruple your hourly spare-time output. Begin using these time-expanders now.

Work everywhere. Learn to work on trains, planes, buses, at home, at dull meetings—everywhere. I travel extensively as part of my regular job. Yet I always bring some spare-time work with me. Once I've finished working for my employer I turn to my spare-time activities. Thus, some of the present book was written while I traveled—on planes, in hotels and motels.

Set aside a space at home for your spare-time work. Even a small desk will do. One of the most successful second-income fortune builders I know began work on a desk made of three orange crates he found in a fruit market. This desk was the only space his wife would allow him in their tiny two-room furnished apartment. Today he owns a $100,000 Park

Avenue duplex apartment and has a large study in which he continues to conduct his successful spare-time business.

In my home I have two studies, each fitted for different business activities. The writing study has two desks, four filing cabinets, and 3,000 reference books. The other study, from which my marine and consulting businesses are operated, is smaller but has similar equipment, including a safe. I spend several hours every evening working in one study or the other.

To work effectively anywhere, get away from noises and interruptions. Keep the equipment you need with you at all times. For most spare-time business activities you need only a few account books, paper and pencil.

"But," you say, "my spare-time business is a vending-machine route. How can I work on it everywhere?" You can't. But you can write checks, analyze sales, plan future routes, and perform similar tasks almost anywhere. Doing this at home will allow you to spend more time checking and servicing your route.

"My social life is too busy—I can't get away from cocktail and bridge parties long enough to do any work at home." I've heard this excuse a thousand times. There's only one answer—take one night a week off from parties. Do all your work then, or devote part of the weekend to work. Anytime Saturday or Sunday will do, if you make a regular practice of working the same number of hours every weekend.

"My wife will scream; there are too many jobs she wants done around the house." Let her scream a few hours a week—she'll purr when you take her downtown to buy the mink or refrigerator she's wanted for so long. For years my wife complained about my book writing and other spare-time activities. Today she keeps after the children while I'm working at home, saying to them, "Don't disturb your father; he's working on an important job." A spare-time dollar—worth two dollars of regular income—will melt the coldest heart. "Money," as the sage said, "answers all things."

Organize your spare time for maximum wealth production. Plan your evenings, your weekends. Know what you intend to do. Then do it. Forget TV for one or two evenings a week. You can live without TV. Try it and see.

Cut back on your hobbies, unless you've made your hobby a business. If you bowl twice a week now, cut back to once a week. Devote the free evening to your business instead of bowling. You'll make money two ways—from your business, and from the bowling fees you save. Of course, one way to enjoy your hobby while earning a spare-time income is to make a hobby your business. Chapter 12 gives many sure-fire hints for combining business and pleasure.

Spend some time with your family, if you have one. But don't spend every moment of your leisure time working around the house, driving the kids to games, or keeping your mother-in-law happy. Insist on having some time to yourself. Devote this time to developing your second-income fortune. Guard against interruptions while you work. Some of my friends lock themselves in their study or basement so they won't be interrupted by children, relatives, or friends.

I have a number of active spare-time businesses which return a good profit. I devote about two hours per evening during the week to my business interests. Over the weekend I may devote another two or three hours to business, depending on what has to be done and how ambitious I am. While I work I concentrate solely on business; I don't stop to watch TV, have a snack, or talk to a neighbor. For I have found that there seem to be hundreds of good reasons for *not* working. If I give into any of these I do not accomplish anything that evening.

Try to finish a task quickly, efficiently. Then go on to your next activity. If you dawdle or delay you lose valuable time, and since time is the capital you'll invest in your first spare-time business, you cannot waste it and expect a profit. Treat and regard your spare time the same way you do money—use time carefully and it will build big profits for you.

Use a written schedule for your spare-time activities, if you can't seem to organize your output in any other way. To do this, buy a diary which devotes a page to each day, with a separate line for each hour. Mark in your diary what you plan to do each day. Check off each task as you complete it. This technique allows you to keep track of your accomplishments. It also allows you to plan future activities.

Some spare-time fortune builders I know use a large wall chart over their desk to keep track of their activities. Others use a looseleaf notebook with a section for each project and a page for each major task.

Choose and use any scheme you like. Just keep in mind the main point—that *you want to organize your spare time for maximum wealth production.* As you increase your hourly income you can either turn to new wealth-building projects or, if you have reached your wealth goal, spend more time on leisure activities. Once you have the spare-time income you desire you can engage in any new activities that interest you, be they business or pleasure. Never waste your fortune-building time.

Get maximum dollar returns for your spare time. Many spare-time fortune builders use a fixed set of rules when considering any new activity. They (1) avoid every business which requires many hours of selling to convince a customer, (2) charge the highest prices possible for personal services, and (3) never perform tasks which someone else will do for a reasonable fee. Let's take a look at each of these rules to see how and why they apply to your spare-time second-income fortune.

(1) In a business where you must spend many hours making a sale, your hourly return will often be low unless the amount of each sale is large. A friend of mine runs a public relations agency in his spare time. He spends so many hours and so much energy looking for clients that he has little time or desire to perform his main task—the preparation of public-relations releases. This experience has led him to conclude that he must find a better business.

Seek the spare-time business in which you can turn every hour of effort into profitable income. Then you won't be wasting time and energy for a low-level income.

(2) When asked to serve as a consultant, teacher, advisor, or witness, many beginners agree to work free of charge or for a very small fee. They do this because they are afraid that if they ask for a large fee the client will not employ them.

It's true that some clients will decline to hire you if they think your fee is too high. But other, better clients will not only hire you but they will have greater respect for you when you insist on a high fee. It took me a long time to realize this. When I first started to teach in my spare time I charged a fee of $5 per hour. Gradually I raised my hourly fee. Today I charge $50 per hour—$1,000 for a 20-hour course. When I charged $5 per hour I had trouble finding people who were willing to hire me. Today, when my rate is $50 per hour, I cannot fulfill all the requests I have to give courses. In fact, at the present time, several firms are on a waiting list for my courses.

So charge a high fee for your services. You may lose a few jobs because your fee is high, but the jobs you get will bring you a higher hourly return. You'll find you're working fewer hours and earning more money.

(3) If you write a book, don't try to type it yourself. You'll waste time on a task that a good typist can do faster and better. This principle applies to many similar tasks such as typing of business letters, preparation of bills and addressing envelopes. Why should you spend your time on these activities when you can be doing other things that will earn you a profit?

Concentrate on earning $25, $50, or $100 per hour. Then you can afford to pay someone $5 to $10 per hour to do work that is below your level of skills. Of course, during your first few months when you have no income, you'll be better off doing these jobs yourself. However, as soon as you can afford to pay someone for these tasks, do so. Freeing your time for more creative work will help you conserve those precious spare-time hours. Then you will truly be making time work for your second-income fortune.

RELATE TIME AND YOUR DOLLAR RETURN

Be ready for a slow start when you begin your first spare-time second-income business. Your business may blossom within a few weeks after you start it—if you're lucky. More likely, however, several months, or even a year, may be needed to build the business volume and profit you desire. Don't worry—most good businesses begin slowly. Be patient; stick with your business if it shows sure, steady growth. Too many beginning spare-time fortune builders give up their pursuit of a second income before they've really made enough effort. So stick with a good idea and it will pay off. You can do anything you want to, if your desire is strong enough.

Keep progress records of your profits. Use a simple accounting system to record your income and expense. If you organize your time for maximum wealth production it will be easy for you to figure your hourly income. Try to make your profits rise as time passes. A business that fails to show a growth in volume and profits may soon be too small to be worth your time. By making regular and careful monthly checks of the progress of your profits, you can soon tell if a given business is worth your time and effort.

Don't allow your profits to stagnate at a low level. When this happens, your profits can only change in one direction—down. In a business where profits stagnate at a *high level* you have two *advantages:* (a) profits are high so your income is good, (b) should profits decrease, you will have time to sell the business at a favorable price because its earnings record has been good. With *low-level* profits you have two *disadvantages:* (a) your income is poor, (b) with a low earnings record you may be unable to sell the business, or may have to take a loss on its sale. When you see that a business has hit the top of its profit potential at a low level, sell it quickly before it acquires a long history of low profits. By selling quickly you may be able to get a good price on the basis of future prospective earnings.

Seek new ways to boost your hourly income. Why be content with $10 an hour when, with a little creative thinking, you could earn $12.50 or $15 per hour? A creative approach to your second-income fortune has many advantages. By using your mind to improve the profits your business earns, you broaden your outlook. This broadened outlook can lead you to new business ideas, new ways to earn greater profits, and ways to reduce your operating costs. Read a few good books on creativity. You'll find them in your local library. These books will give you many ideas for stimulating the creative powers of your mind.

Diversify your interests and efforts. Dr. Howell T. Lykes, founder of Lykes Brothers Steamship Company, Inc., was a physician who became interested in raising cattle. From this business he diversified to shipping, import-export, and numerous sidelines. The business he founded expanded to include many other activities—ranch lands, citrus fruit orchards, meat packing, stevedoring, a sand and gravel mine, an insurance company, an electronics company, a reforestation project, a hotel, and a cattle-feeding project.

Diversifying your interests and efforts can open new fields to you. This will enable you to obtain a greater return from every hour you spend in your spare-time second-income business. You will also increase your business knowledge and skills. While most successful second-income fortune builders start with only one business, many develop three or four other profitable businesses as their income and experience increase. Having more than one business can raise your profits while protecting you from a total loss of income if one business fails.

USE MODERN TIME-SAVERS TO MAXIMIZE PROFITS

Never be afraid to spend a dollar to save or earn two or more dollars. If you must dictate large amounts of information in your spare-time business, buy a dictating machine. There are excellent units available for less than $200. A good dictating machine will save you time and earn back its cost in a few months.

Investigate pick-up secretarial services if you must write many letters. Most areas have a secretarial service which will pick up correspondence on a daily or weekly basis. Your letters will be typed from dictating-machine tapes, longhand notes, or form replies. The charge is nominal.

Use your telephone to boost your income. Call customers, suppliers, dealers, and others to keep a tighter control on your business. A phone call can often save an expensive, time-consuming business trip. Ask your local phone company for their booklet on doing business over the phone. Most phone companies supply these booklets free of charge and are delighted to advise you on how to improve the efficiency of your business contacts by using the telephone.

Make full use of telegrams, air mail, special-delivery mail, and similar aids. They cost a little more but these aids get your message across faster and more effectively. Seek free advice from the telegraph company and United States Post Office. You'll learn many useful procedures. And you'll find that the extra cost is small compared with the efficiency and effectiveness of these modern aids. They'll help you get more income from every spare-time hour.

BE PROFESSIONAL AND EARN MORE FROM YOUR TIME

Should you have an office for your spare-time business? Much depends on the type of business you conduct, and the attitude of your family towards it. If clients *must* visit you to transact business then an office will pay for itself. But if you normally are expected to call on clients then an office probably isn't necessary.

Is your family sympathetic to your business activities? Do your wife and children permit you to work at home without interruption, or are they always popping into your study to ask questions or discuss the latest satellite launching? If you can't find peace and quiet at home, then you need an office in which to work. An uninterrupted hour in an office can be far more productive than several hours at home with almost constant interruption.

A young, beginning second-income fortune builder I know couldn't afford to rent an office. So he worked at his local library until his income rose to a level where he could afford office rent. To work efficiently in the library he brought an attache case with him. In the case he had all the necessary papers and equipment to do business. When necessary, he used the reference books in th   ary as sources of business information. Other beginning fortune builders I know started their careers in a quiet corner of a cafeteria. By keeping a cup of coffee in front of them they were able to occupy a table for several hours. "Coffee," as one successful second-income fortune builder comments, "costs less than rent. Also, it keeps you alert."

Another wealthy friend started a spare-time accounting business at home. He soon acquired a long list of clients. But his wife and children kept hindering him—he couldn't add a column of figures without some member of his family barging in. He rented a small one-room office for $50 per month and today his business is booming. One unexpected advantage of the office was the many prospective clients he met in the building where his office is located.

In large cities you can rent desk space by the hour, day, week, month, or year. Telephone and mail service are also available, if you wish. The desk gives you a quiet place to work, often at a "prestige" address—that is, a desirable area in the business section. Desk-space rates are usually lower than rent.

Get a business phone and employ an answering service if your clients will call you frequently. Have the phone listed under your business name in both the regular directory and the yellow pages of the telephone book. Your business will be more highly respected and you'll get calls from prospective clients who find your name in the yellow pages. One of my business phones is listed in both these directories. Several clients who've learned about me from the yellow pages have given me assignments having fees large enough to pay my phone bills for the next fifty years. So don't scrimp on phone service—you can lose valuable business while trying to save a few dollars.

Devise an attractive letterhead and calling card for your business. Have a supply printed by a competent printing house. If you can't design a suitable letterhead, have the printer do it for you, or hire an industrial designer; the fee is modest compared with the results you'll obtain. A professional looking letterhead makes every letter you write attract attention, assuring you a better return from every spare-time hour you spend on business. Use your letterhead *and* business card for *every* business letter you write and business call you make. Why go to the expense of preparing good business materials and then forget to use them? Remember: your letter and card represent you when you're not around. Make them good—and use them.

Keep neat files and records of all your business transactions. You can purchase easy-to-use account books at your local stationery store. Get these books and begin keeping records of income and expenses from the first moment you get an idea for a business.

I maintain very accurate account books for my many business activities. To be certain every expense is recorded I carry a small expense and tax record book with me at all times. In this I enter every cent I spend, from ten cents for a newspaper to thirty or forty dollars for reference books. This record tells me how much it costs to do business and is helpful when I prepare my income-tax return.

Buy a small filing cabinet for your business correspondence, purchase orders, bills, and other papers. If you can't afford a metal cabinet, get a corrugated cardboard "transfer file." These cost only a few dollars and will last several years. Keep a three-by-five-inch card file cabinet on your desk if you must have records of many small bits of information such as customers' names and addresses. The three-by-five cards are easy to carry with you and are handy for recording notes and other information.

Be neat in all your business activities—letters, records, bills, orders and receipts. Think of the last time you had a small businessman do some work for you—say, having your car tuned up. Weren't you impressed by a neat, clean, shiny shop? Didn't you have greater confidence in a neatly dressed mechanic whose tools were carefully arranged and ready for use? Certainly you did. The same applies in your business. Your clients and customers will keep coming back if they are impressed with your neatness and efficiency.

Keep your office, shop, or store clean, neat, ready for instant use. Insist that your letters and bills be clearly and neatly typed. Refuse to accept smudged typing, excessive erasures. Be sure that every bill you send is accurate and clear. Make every piece of paper that comes from your business a personal representative of yourself—for that's what it is. Build an image of accuracy and efficiency and you won't have enough time or energy to serve the customers who seek you out. Neatness and efficiency build the effectiveness of your spare-time efforts.

A professional approach to your spare-time business has another major advantage: it gives you the maximum legal deductions for income-tax purposes. By being able to *claim* and *prove* your business expenses you can lower the taxes on the income you earn. Thus, you'll have more of your spare-time dollar left on the day after your tax return is due.

SECRETS OF GETTING MORE PROFIT FROM EVERY HOUR

Here, for the first time anywhere, are my secrets for building a second-income spare-time fortune. Using these secrets built many successful businesses for me. They enabled me to purchase a large, comfortable home, keep two new automobiles in my driveway, cruise in a comfortable powerboat, dive to the bottom of the sea with my own diving apparatus, give my children an excellent education, pay for a large insurance policy and the best medical care, and travel to many countries. You can do the same, or other things, if you apply these secrets for getting more from every spare-time hour. Here are the three easy-to-use secrets.

1. *Motivate yourself.* Don't wait for someone to urge you to build a second-income spare-time fortune. *Make the desire spring from within yourself.*

Motivate yourself with the rewards money brings—a new car, a bigger home, a set of golf clubs. Use your desires for material possessions as a spur to greater spare-time efforts. Don't strain so much that you have a rushed, pushed feeling in your spare time. Instead, work at a steady, comfortable pace to achieve your goals. Plan your time carefully. Reward yourself with some time off whenever you reach a major milestone on the road to your goal.

Spoil yourself now and then by just being lazy for a day or two. Buy yourself a treasured item when an unusually large payment comes in. Above all keep your motivation clearly in view at all times. Push towards your goal every day, even if the pushing involves only thinking about your objective. Prefer a slow, steady, productive pace to a hurried, harried, wheel-spinning grind. Make every minute, every hour, a step on your road to a spare-time second-income fortune.

2. *Visualize your rewards.* Keep your motivating drives in mind at all times. Visualize the rewards you will obtain today, tomorrow, and in the long-range future. Make your rewards the fuel that propels you to an outstanding future. Blast off and stay in orbit. Keep pictures of your objective in front of you while you work. If you aim at a high-powered sports car, cut a picture out of a catalog. House, ranch, boat, vacation, stocks motivate you? Get pictures of what you want and hang them in front of your desk, slip them under the glass on your desk, or paste them inside a handy drawer. Look at them often and visualize how you'll feel when you own the things you want. Then work steadily to achieve your rewards. For as E. W. Scripps, the self-made newspaper millionaire, wrote, "A man can do anything he wants to do in this world if he wants to badly enough." Man or woman, you can do the same—if you visualize your rewards and work for them.

3. *Make fortune-building part of your life pattern.* Don't limit your second-income spare-time fortune building to only 7:00 to 8:00 P.M. on weekday evenings. Think about your fortune every hour of the day. Be constantly alert for new income schemes, new tax-saving ideas, ways in which you can expand your profits. This alertness will help you expand your fortune while providing you with useful ideas for your steady job.

Work regular hours while building your second-income spare-time fortune. Make fortune building a part of every day of your life. Follow a planned schedule and your fortune will grow steadily and surely. Check on results regularly. Then you will know that you are making time work for your spare-time second-income fortune.

You are now ready to begin the actual building of your spare-time second-income fortune. If you've read this book carefully up to this chapter you have subtly built up strong enthusiasm and go-power to begin the job of building your fortune. Let's get started immediately.

If you don't have much money to begin your hunt for a fortune, don't despair; few people start with a big bankroll. What's more, you're probably better off starting with only a few dollars and little experience.

Should you have $100,000 to invest in

9

Begin with

Low-Capital

Modest-Time Ventures

a business, would your chances for success be much greater than if you have $100? No; they wouldn't. Why? Because with a large bankroll you'd try to begin a big business—possibly with a factory, some trucks, and an expensive payroll to meet. This is an excellent way to go broke—fast—if you have little experience.

Starting with low capital you stand just as much chance of going broke, but losing $100, $1,000, or $3,000 won't be as damaging to you as losing a large sum of money. Also, when you begin a low-capital business you can't afford to hire anyone to do the nasty jobs. So you must do them all yourself. The result is that you learn every part of the business. When your income rises to a level which enables you to hire someone, you are better able to direct his activities. Your chances for continued success are greater. So don't moan about a lack of capital—get started on building your second-income fortune as soon as possible.

At the start, time is cheaper than money to you. Make your time serve in the place of money wherever possible. Then you will be able to save your capital for those items which cannot be bought with your time. Remember that when you reduce your money investment and substitute time in its place, you will have to spend many hours on your business; but the amount of time you invest is modest compared to your potential returns. Using time in place of money also shows you the fair rate of pay for employees you hire in the future.

PROFITABLE ZERO-CAPITAL VENTURES

Here are seven powerful ideas for ventures requiring no capital investment of any kind, other than time. Perhaps one of these spare-time second-income businesses will interest you or will suggest another zero-capital venture you'd like to try. Read each description carefully—it may be your path to financial freedom.

1. *Mutual-fund salesman.* Part-time mutual-fund salesmen earn as high as $25 per hour during every hour they sell. You need not have a special education—many mutual funds don't care if you've graduated from high school—provided you make a neat appearance, talk well, and are interested in selling. If you live in a large city a mutual fund will train you, free of charge, in evening classes. For those who aren't near a large city, some mutual funds will train you by means of a simple correspon-

dence course. All materials, including your course, sales kit, stationery, and calling cards are supplied free of charge. Should you consider this lucrative spare-time second-income business? Yes, you should, if you like selling and if you have a wide circle of friends or acquaintances. What kind of occupation makes a good combination with mutual funds? Here are a few: gas-station owner or attendant, elevator operator, member of the armed forces (Army, Navy, Air Force, Marine Corps, Coast Guard), insurance salesman, store owner. The key is any job where you meet the public in large numbers, providing an excellent source of potential clients for spare-time mutual-fund sales. The mutual funds are constantly seeking thousands of new salesmen and saleswomen.

2. *Business finder.* To become a successful business finder all you need are alert eyes, sharp ears, and intense curiosity about other people's business. What does a finder do? He *finds* businesses for someone, usually the president of a firm or an independent businessman. What kind of business would you find? Almost any kind. Thus, you might find an idea for a new product, a firm that wishes to merge with another, a market for a product, a new manufacturing process, a useful patent, a piece of real estate needed by a company. To work as a finder you need only learn which items firms and businessmen are looking for and willing to pay cash for. Your payment may be a fixed sum per unit of product sold, such as ten cents per pound of steel. Or you may receive a fixed percentage of the list price of a product—say 3 percent of list on items up to $100. Some firms prefer to pay a flat fee. These fees can range as high as $150,000.

If you write for money, either in your spare time or as your regular occupation, or if you know a number of authors, you can be a publisher's finder. Many book publishers pay a finder's fee for authors you bring to them. This fee may be a lump-sum payment or a royalty percentage on each copy of the author's book which the publisher sells.

To get a start as a finder, study the Equipment Wanted and similar columns of your business newspapers and trade journals. Then try to locate a seller of such equipment. After locating the equipment, contact the firm wanting it. Offer to supply the equipment either at a price which includes your fee, or arrange a special fee. You can use this technique for many items other than equipment.

You may benefit by joining a finder's club. One, Finderhood, Inc., issues regular reports and bulletins listing the immediate needs of many companies and individuals. If you fill one of these needs the club protects your interests and sees that you receive the full finder's fee listed in the club's bulletin. These fees can range from a few hundred dollars to many thousands of dollars.

Successful, lucrative finding costs you little and can bring you a fortune. Give serious consideration to becoming a finder if you have a specialized knowledge of any subject or business, or know a large number of business people. A good friend of mine is currently finding a suitable company to merge with another one. Devoting only Saturday mornings to the project, he located a suitable company. His fee will be 7 per cent of the merger price; the current price is $6 million, which will give him a fee of $420,000. This is a nice return for spare-time work on Saturday.

3. *Political patronage income.* If you like politics there's a good chance you can get a "patronage" job in your local area. These jobs are generally given to political campaign workers—district captains, speakers, leaflet distributors, sign painters. Thus, in one eastern city a street inspector, who spends his spare time looking for holes in streets and checking patched holes, is paid $1,800 per year. He works when he chooses, uses city-supplied forms to report his findings by mail. Since the street is his "office" he never has to punch a time clock or check into a plant. His only investment is shoe leather and a ballpoint pen. This street inspector is pyramiding his income; instead of spending the $1,800 he's investing it in another business. Other patronage jobs include election inspectors ($10 to $25 per day), city marshal, town sheriff, and process server. If you wish to qualify for a patronage job, become more active in your local political party. Do a good job and someone is sure to recommend you for a part-time job.

4. *No-down-payment real estate.* You can buy raw land and rental property with no money down if you keep a careful watch on the real estate columns of your newspapers. Visit a few active real estate offices and tell the agent what you're looking for—either land or rental property with no down payment. It may take awhile, but you're almost certain to have several suitable properties offered to you.

Decide in advance what you want to do. If you wish to speculate, buy raw land. Then make every effort you can to sell it at a higher price than you agreed to pay for it. Clyde T. Cadwallader, a highly successful real estate operater, made his first investment in 100 acres of land. He sold four parcels of the tract before closing *his* purchase of the land. His eventual profit was about $2,000.

To be a successful land speculator you must be able to visualize what can be done with a given piece of property *after* you take it over. Then you must go out and find customers for the property. Don't speculate in land if you want to just sit back and wait for buyers to come to you. Successful land speculators visualize the potential for a property, actively seek customers, and convince potential customers that the property meets their needs. If such a program appeals to you, try your luck on one or two no-down-payment deals. Your return can be very high.

No-down-payment rental property is usually a one-, two-, or three-family dwelling in which you do not live. You rent the entire building to one or more families. Try to avoid one-family rental dwellings unless you intend to operate a number of such units, possibly five or more. With two-family or larger dwellings you have a better chance of meeting mortgage payments out of rent because you will seldom have a situation where all the apartments are vacant at the same time. If you lose a tenant from a one-family dwelling you must make the mortgage payments out of other income. With five or more rental homes the profits from the occupied dwellings will usually be enough for the mortgage payment on one unoccupied building.

Check your local Real Estate Sales, House-Wanted ads, and real estate agent before purchasing any rental property. To ensure a successful start, wait until there is a strong demand for apartments or homes, depending on the type of property you plan to buy. If you buy when rental demands are low you may be stuck with high mortgage payments and no income.

To find no-down-payment real estate read several local papers *every* day. Study the real estate columns carefully. You may have to wait several months to find the type of property you want. Be patient, sooner or later the ad you are looking for will appear. Act on it immediately, calling or writing the seller. Figure your potential cash profits as shown below. The building in this example has ten 4-room apartments and ten single-car garages.

ANNUAL BUILDING CASH STATEMENT

Apartment Rents (10 apartments each @ $100 per month)		$12,000
Garage Rents (10 garages each @ $30 per month)		3,600
Gross rental income		15,600
Operating Costs		
Building maintenance and repairs	$1,050	
Real estate taxes on land and building	850	
Insurance (fire and liability)	750	
Electricity (lobby, basement, elevator)	500	
Water-use fee	50	
Labor (superintendent and handyman)	3,600	
Total operating costs	6,800	
Interest on mortgage	950	
Mortgage principal	3,600	
Interest and mortgage costs	4,550	
Total annual operating and mortgage costs		11,350
Annual cash income from building and garages		$4,250

The income shown here is also called M.I.F.—money-in-fist—because it is the actual cash you have at the end of the year. Depreciation allowances will usually increase your *on-paper income* but won't put any money in your pocket. For this reason, all experienced real estate fortune builders put most emphasis on the M.I.F. of a property.

5. Be a consultant. To be a successful consultant you need only three items at the start. Two of these items are in most homes—a telephone and a desk. The third item is in your head. It is specialized knowledge of one or more subjects. These subjects can be almost anything, from acorns to zippers. Somewhere in this great country of ours, someone is probably willing to pay you money for your specialized knowledge about the subject. Of course, your chances of becoming a highly paid spare-time consultant are much better if your specialized knowledge is related to a business subject. However, the smart spare-time second-income fortune builder develops ways in which he can adapt his specialized knowledge to business situations.

Once you've decided to become a consultant in a given area of knowledge, your next task is to find clients. There are a number of ways to do this. Some consultants watch the Help Wanted ads. When they see an ad for someone having their knowledge they offer their services on a consulting basis. This is often a successful approach in areas of knowledge and experience where there is a shortage of trained personnel. Other consultants write articles on their specialty. They receive a payment for the article from the magazine that publishes it. More important, however, the consultant's name is publicized among the readers of the magazine. If the article is important to the readers of the magazine, the consultant may receive inquiries about the cost of his services. Many consultants obtain excellent clients this way. Some consultants regard the acquisition of clients as far more important than the article payment they receive from the magazine. But when you first start you will probably welcome the article payment as useful spare-time income.

There are many other ways to publicize your consulting activities. Thus, you can volunteer to do free consulting for your city or town, for your religious group, for a fraternal organization, and similar groups. You can also become a member of a committee of the society or association representing your particular specialty. Consulting jobs will often be offered to you because of your position on the committee.

Today is an age of specialization. More consultants with more highly specialized knowledge are needed today than ever before in our history. If you have a good knowledge of a particular subject, or can acquire such knowledge, you have an excellent chance of building a lucrative spare-time second-income fortune by becoming a consultant. Here are a dozen random specialities in which consultants are needed today: marketing, pleasure boating, rental property, automotive operating costs, technical writing, small-business operation, education of senior citizens, retirement occupations, specialized electronics businesses, church fund drives, automation, and profitable accounting procedures. Use this list as a guide to specialties in which *you* can consult. Your daily fees for seven hours of consulting work will range between $100 and $500, depending on the specialty and number of clients available.

6. *Field representatives can earn big money.* Thousands of firms in the United States would be delighted to appoint you, free of charge, as one of their field representatives. In this capacity you will represent the company, selling its products at a nice profit to yourself. The company

gives you a good discount on its products—usually 20 per cent or more—and you sell the product at its full list price. Any needed supplies like order blanks, return envelopes, customer data sheets, are usually furnished to you free. You can list yourself as Field Representative, the XYZ Company.

Where can you find customers for the products you sell? Almost everywhere—on your regular job, in your neighborhood, in your religious group, in your club. What kinds of products might you sell? There are hundreds, such as technical books, specialized magazines, hobby equipment, home maintenance devices. To learn of the many opportunities, study the display and classified ads of magazines serving the field in which you are interested. You will also find good leads in magazines like *Popular Science, Popular Mechanics,* and others aimed at a predominantly male readership. If you prefer, you can write or visit the firms you wish to represent. They will be happy to provide the information you need to get started.

7. *Other zero-capital ventures.* You now know the general approach to zero-capital ventures: either use your existing talents and facilities to begin a business, or find a company to finance your activities. Other part-time ventures you might wish to study are selling automobiles, boats, houses, motorcycles, and similar products in the evenings and on weekends; teaching in your local adult-education program; serving as a juror, fireman, policeman, judge, sheriff, mayor, or other official in your community (J. M. Kirby, who became a millionaire through his real estate holdings, was mayor of Wyoming, Ohio, while operating a highly successful real estate business); writing articles, stories, or books for publication; producing publicity material for small companies, clubs, churches, and similar organizations; freelance photography, manuscript editing, or drafting; teaching golf, tennis, bowling, swimming, diving, or any of many other sports; working as a painter, plumber, waiter, usher, salesman, TV repairman, or in any other service field; or teaching music, foreign languages, painting, or ceramics. Fred Lee, the oil millionaire, began his fortune by claiming survey vacancies (overlooked land) in the West Texas Yates Oilfield. These claims cost almost nothing. Lee's good sense was soon proven when many producing wells were found on his claims.

If your zero-capital venture is a part-time job, you may regard it as the first step on your way to a second-income business; or you may choose to regard the job as *your* source of a satisfying second income. Make your own decision—you won't lose either way. With a spare-time job you'll be receiving a steady, extra income. As a first step towards a second-income business you'll be building cash for a low-capital modest-time venture.

LOW-CAPITAL MODEST-TIME VENTURES

In these ventures you invest some of your savings to either buy or start a spare-time second-income business. Why should I pay to buy or start a business when I can begin to earn *without* any investment, you ask. There are several good reasons why you should *consider* investing some money. Here they are.

(1) With money invested in a business you work harder to protect your investment while making it grow. Your chances for success are greater. (2) Investing in a business gives you a different outlook from the one accompanying a business without an investment. You become a more careful worker; you investigate every step before you take it; you are truly a businessman. (3) In general, better businesses are available to investors with some ready cash. This doesn't mean that it is impossible to get a good business without investing some cash. What it does mean is that a business you acquire by making a cash investment is usually more mature; it requires less effort from you to generate a consistently good profit.

Where can you invest a small amount of money to earn a good return for your spare-time second-income fortune? Here are six good business areas that are lucrative to many spare-time fortune builders: (1) real estate, (2) neighborhood services, (3) personal services, (4) specialty manufacturing, (5) stock, money, and commodity markets, and (6) overseas business. Let's take a quick look at each.

RENTAL REAL ESTATE

There are many excellent apartment buildings available throughout the United States for a cash investment of $1,000 to $50,000. These buildings will return an income from less than $1,000 per year to more than $10,000 per year, depending on their location, condition, number of apartments, existence of rent control, and the type of tenants you choose.

You can find buildings of this type by working through a real estate agent and following the ads in your local papers. The usual price of these buildings is five to nine times the annual *gross* income (i.e., income from all rental spaces *before* any bills are paid).

Before investing any money in rental property, keep these facts in mind. *Location* is a prime factor in all real estate—prefer a run-down building in a good location to a new building in a seamy neighborhood that has no future. Good locations are near cheap (bus, subway) transportation, may have attractive scenic views (hills, lakes, rivers), are near shopping facilities, have a "prestige" address, or are near a constant source of tenants (school, college, or industrial plant). Of course, few locations possess all these advantages; most have only one, or possibly two. A. M. Sonnabend built a multimillion-dollar fortune in real estate and many other diverse hotel and business activities by starting with $5,000 in *borrowed* capital. During his first year he made a profit of $22,000. Sonnabend always gave great thought to location in every real estate deal he made.

Condition of the building is next in importance to location. A run-down fire trap may be cheap to buy but can be a headache forever. Your insurance costs in such a building can be sky-high. If the building burns down or collapses you may have a large lawsuit to fight. I always avoid old, neglected buildings in my real-estate ventures and concentrate on newer or better-maintained structures. In this way I avoid large repair bills and other profit-eating expenses. Many of my successful friends follow a similar plan. They reason that a few dollars less profit on a higher-cost newer building is much better than a slightly higher profit on a risky structure that may kill tenants by burning up or falling down.

Class of tenants makes a big difference in collecting rents. In general, it is easier to collect rents from true apartment dwellers—people who want to live in an apartment instead of a home of their own. These people, who are usually in the lower-income brackets, take pride in paying their rent on time every month. The ideal family of this type has one or two teenage children; the parents are in their forties or fifties. Their income is at a high level and they have no trouble meeting the monthly rent payment. Avoid, if you can, young, single people trying to get ahead fast. They may change apartments quickly, leaving unpaid rent bills behind.

Unheated buildings are excellent rental properties because you are relieved of furnace attendance, fuel bills, and maintenance. Some buildings in the east and far west have separate heating units for each apartment. These are ideal because the tenant pays his own heating bill and you are relieved of all complaints about the apartments being too hot or too cold. The tenant adjusts his own thermostat and curses it instead of you.

Other items you must consider before buying any rental apartments are: Who will maintain the building (handyman, superintendent, maintenance firm)? How much will maintenance cost each year? How will you collect rents (by mail is best way)? Who will shovel snow in the winter if the building is in a snow area? Who will advertise and show apartments to prospective tenants? How will heating oil or coal be ordered? Are there any closing fees when you buy the building? If so, how much are they? What about a title search? What are typical insurance costs for the building?

If rental property appeals to you as a part-time second-income business, begin today to search for a suitable building. You can earn an excellent income with relatively little investment of money or time if the price of the building is not greater than five to seven times the annual income. Before buying any building be certain to have it inspected and appraised by a competent appraiser. Never sign any papers until *after* you receive the appraiser's report. To be sure the building is what you want and is in good condition go along with the appraiser or check the building yourself. Be alert and use all your senses while inspecting the building. Don't be stuck by a shrewd operator or a careless appraiser.

Industrial buildings, generally, are not as attractive for spare-time operation as apartment houses. The usual industrial building has only one tenant and if he moves out you may have a difficult time meeting the mortgage payments. While many industrial buildings are leased for long periods—often 10 years or more—these are usually large structures that are too expensive for the beginning part-time fortune builder. So stay away from industrial buildings until you have sufficient experience and capital.

Rental real estate can give you a steady, profitable spare-time second income. Several typical examples of real estate investments are given earlier in this book. Study these as a guide to your own ventures. Keep two facts in mind for all rental real estate: (1) Never tie up too much of your capital in an investment which is difficult to sell—and most rental property takes at least a month to sell. So keep some cash handy because you usually won't be able to sell a rental property quickly. (2) With money invested in a rental property your mortgage payments are lower. This means that your profits will be higher than if you bought the property with no money down.

TRY LEASING REAL ESTATE

Some owners of real estate do not want to sell their property. They'd prefer to lease it at a fixed annual charge for a specified number of years. You can lease to others if you own real estate, or you can lease land or buildings from others and use it to produce income. Let's look at each situation.

Suppose you own land in the business section of town. An oil company offers to buy the land from you. But you don't want to sell the property. So you offer to lease the land to the company. Such a lease can run from five years to ninety-five years. Each year you collect a fixed annual fee. When the lease expires the land reverts to you. The company leasing the land erects suitable structures for their business and removes them before the lease expires. A good friend of mine earns a profitable spare-time second income by leasing several excellent gasoline-station sites in down-town Los Angeles to various oil companies. You can, of course, also lease buildings to desirable tenants.

Let's say you've bought land or buildings that are in a part of town zoned "industrial," meaning factories can operate there. How do you make it pay? Here's one way that works well.

Study the property and decide what it's best suited for—light industry like product assembly, plastics manufacture, sheet-metal fabrication; marine activities, if located along a river or creek; commercial purposes if in a shopping area. Advertise in newspapers and trade journals serving the types of industry that might use your property. Offer inducements, such as the first three months free, alteration of buildings, or construction of roads, to firms that will sign a long lease. Be certain that your first year's lease fee will at least pay for the cost of any changes you make. After that your lease fee must pay all taxes and other charges on the property, *plus* your profit.

If you can find a responsible company to lease your property *before* you buy it, a bank may be willing to finance the complete purchase price of the property, plus the cost of any necessary improvements. Your key here is finding a company with a good enough credit rating to be acceptable to the bank. Strange as it seems, there are many such companies interested in leasing the *right* piece of property for them. In some cases they will lease property for periods up to thirty years. If you want, you can arrange the lease so that the tenant pays all the property maintenance expenses during the life of the lease.

Leasing your property has many important advantages. For example, you are assured of a fixed, steady income for a specified period. Furthermore, property in a good location will probably increase in value during the life of the lease. With one or more buildings on the property, depreciation deductions can markedly reduce the income taxes on the profits. Thus, you have more income for your own use. Chapter 14 gives you many powerful tax pointers useful in your real estate activities. Now let's look at the reverse of this leasing procedure, where *you* lease property from others.

Assume you want to operate an apartment house for income production, but you'd prefer not to tie up any cash in real estate. How can you arrange a deal? It's simple. Watch your local papers for apartment houses advertised as available for lease. Such ads appear every month or so in larger cities. If you don't see an ad like this, watch for a regular sales ad that runs for several weeks. Contact the owner, offering a lease instead of a purchase. Your offer may be accepted.

When you lease property or buildings you have several advantages. The lease fee is directly deductible as a business expense on your income tax. In addition, legal fees for arranging a lease are usually much less than for purchase of the same property. If you lease a building or structure during the middle years of its life, you will be turning it back to the owner at a time when its maintenance costs are beginning to rise. These costs become the owner's headache, not yours. You can do almost anything you want with the property to earn an income from it, provided you restore it to its original condition before the lease expires. Thus, you can rent out individual apartments, sub-lease the entire building or plot, or take any of many other similar steps to earn a profit from the property.

Either way your lease can put dollars in your pocket. However, before leasing any property be completely certain that the potential income exceeds the leasing costs by a factor of 3-to-1. Thus, if you pay $1,000 per year to lease a building, you should have a gross income of at least $3,000 per year to show a reasonable profit for your spare-time efforts. You might even aim at 4-to-1, but be happy with 3-to-1.

OTHER REAL ESTATE VENTURES

There are hundreds of other ways to earn a good spare-time income from real estate. These include ownership and operation or leasing of motels, hotels, parking lots, gas stations, supermarkets, shopping centers, marinas, dry cleaning centers, auto cleaners, and similar properties. With each of these you obtain the two big advantages of real estate investment —the leverage resulting from your having much less cash invested in the property than the mortgage holder does, and the tax advantages of depreciation of buildings and equipment. Depreciation requires no cash investment but measurably increases your cash income. An excellent guide to the many ways of earning good profits from real estate ventures is William J. Casey's "Real Estate Desk Book," Institute for Business Planning, Inc., New York. Obtain a copy of this book and study it thoroughly. In it you will find many fine discussions and examples of topics important to every spare-time real estate investor. Another helpful book by the same author and publisher is "Real Estate Investments and How to Make Them."

NEIGHBORHOOD SERVICES CAN BE GOLD MINES

You, like all of us, live in a neighborhood of some kind. This neighborhood may be in a city, a town, or the country. Your neighbors, as people everywhere, need many services. Perhaps you can supply some of these services in your spare time at a profit. Arnold Palmer, the champion golfer and highly successful operator of several golf-related businesses, is also president of a neighborhood service business—the Arnold Palmer Laundries, Dry Cleaning and Maid Service, Inc.

What kinds of service businesses can you enter by investing some capital and your time? There are many, including low-cost coin laundries, taverns, appliance repair, TV and radio repair, gasoline service stations, building repair, building cleaning, weekend (two-day) restaurants or doughnut stores, vending machines, ice-cream distribution, taxicab operation, store self-service displays, beauty-parlor operation, laminating with plastics, collecting bills, insurance sales, gardening and garden supplies, auto tuneup, auto cleaning, printed products (letterheads, business cards, envelopes), custom costume jewelry, selling antiques, operating a bill-paying agency for individuals or small businesses, cleaning and refurbishing furniture, building furniture, reweaving clothes and fabrics, giving financial advice to individuals and small business concerns, teaching special skills (bookkeeping, tax procedures, sports, hobbies), caring for pets (dogs, cats, birds), cosmetics sales, uniform laundering and care, pastry sales, rug cleaning and repair, piano tuning, health-food selling, travel-agency operation, and hundreds of others.

How much capital do you need for a neighborhood service business? You can obtain a beginning costume jewelry kit for only $25. If you want to clean rugs and upholstery by operating from your home, the needed equipment can be bought for about $500. Doughnut stores or kitchens can be started for as little as $3,500. You can buy many coin laundries, beauty parlors, barber shops, and taverns in suburban areas with $3,000 to $5,000 cash down payment. The full price, which you can pay out of business earnings, runs $8,000 to $15,000 in most areas. For $250,000 you can open a luxurious coin-operated dry-cleaning and laundry center. So you see, you can start a neighborhood service business with as little or as much cash as you want to invest.

How do you start a neighborhood service business? You take these twelve steps:

1. Study your neighborhood's service needs.
2. Find one or more needs that are not being met.
3. Make a careful survey of the number of potential customers.
4. Estimate the potential income from filling the need.
5. Determine the number of hours you must devote to the business.
6. Compute the amount of capital you'll need.
7. Decide where you'll operate the business—home or store.
8. Prepare a "dry-run" plan for the first year's activities.
9. Study this plan for possible trouble spots.
10. Allow a few days to pass; then make your decision.
11. Investigate a similar business in another area.
12. Invest your money if the "dry run" and investigation are favorable.

Taking these twelve steps will prevent you from rushing into a business about which you know nothing. Your study of your neighborhood's service needs will reveal which services are not being supplied. There's little sense of opening another gas station in a small town already having three stations, unless there is a special traffic situation which might support a new station. You'd probably be much better off opening a tavern, restaurant, coin laundry, or a similar business, if such a service does not now exist in the town. Since you cannot devote too many hours to your spare-time service business you want to be certain your efforts will be rewarded with a good income.

10

The town I live in has many modern homes, most of which have large, painted kitchen and bathroom cabinets. A few years ago, a friend of mine, Bob P., bought a fifty dollar paint sprayer to refinish the cabinets in his home. Bob, who is a meticulous engineer, spent several weeks refinishing the cabinets. He used a dazzling enamel, spraying each cabinet a bright color selected by his wife. The day after he finished the paint job his wife's bridge club met in his home. The ladies were astounded by the new look given the

Secrets That Make

Low-Capital Investments
Pay Off

kitchen and bathroom by the bright, dazzling colors. They "just had to have" their cabinets refinished, and they all voted that Bob was the only painter in town who could do the job.

Bob studied the town's high-quality painting needs. He found that no one in town could do this sort of work. Yet there were thousands of homes having a total of many thousands of cabinets needing refinishing. If he worked ten hours a week he estimated he could earn $100 per week. Since his materials cost would be low he could show a profit of $3500 to $3800 per year by operating from his home. Word-of-mouth advertising would give him a steady flow of customers. As his last step, Bob checked several nearby towns and found a few painters who earned a good income doing similar work. This convinced him that high-quality cabinet painting would provide a lucrative income. Bob went into business in his spare time. Today he employs three part-time painters and is building an impressive second-income fortune—specializing in a neighborhood service. With his three employees, his spare-time income now exceeds his most optimistic estimates.

Where can *you* get ideas for neighborhood service businesses? Everywhere—at home or away from home. Study your neighborhood carefully every day of the week, and on weekends. Within a few weeks you will almost certainly find two or three needs that are unfilled. Be alert while you travel and when you are on vacation. A service that is successful in another town may also be needed in your town or city. An idea that pays off in California may be just as successful in North Carolina, Maine, New York, or Florida.

Study your local newspaper; many service businesses will be advertised for sale as owners retire or move to new areas. List your income needs and interests with several local business brokers. If you live near a large city, attend the annual business shows held there. One, the "Start Your Own Business" show, will give you many excellent and profitable ideas for a neighborhood service business.

PERSONAL SERVICES CAN PAY BIG PROFITS

If you like people and enjoy dealing with them, you can turn your spare time into a lucrative income by rendering a personal service of some kind. What's more, your capital investment need not be large—you can start with as little as $100. Here are fifty-three personal services that can pay you big profits in your spare time. Some are unusual services that are not found in typical towns and small cities. These personal services are included in this list to stimulate your imagination and creativity. Remember: you need only a good idea to jog you into finding a unique service for your town or city. Now glance at this list:

Auctioneer (real estate, furniture, houses)
Basket filling for gifts and prizes
Car and limousine rental
Diving instruction
Electrolysis for hair removal
Fishing-reel repair and overhaul
Floor waxing (homes and offices)
Fur consultant for women
Furniture polishing in home and office
Gold-leaf application and decoration
Golf instruction on course and indoors
Gymnastic instruction in home and gym
Hair stylist and hair-piece consultant
Handbag design and repair
Home budgeting advice
Instruction in business and hobby skills
Landscaping for home and business
Language teaching at home
Lawn spraying and care
Leasing of personal equipment
Leather-goods design and repair
Lecturing before local groups
Letter writing and remailing
Linen supply and cleaning
Lip-reading instruction
Locksmith services (home and business)
Mail-order sales to individuals
Massage for health and relaxation
Mirror design and cutting
Notary public
Out-of-print and rare books
Personal loans to homeowners
Personal publicity for local people
Private investigation for individuals
Proofreading for publishers
Purchasing services for individuals
Puzzle solving for business and pleasure

Quilting for custom designs
Rabbit and other animal breeding
Rack merchandise service
Reading-improvement training
Real estate appraisal
Real estate management
Real estate renting agency
Religious goods sales
Rental library for general books
Report writing (individuals and business)
Resale or second-hand store
Research bureau (individuals and business)
Stenographic services
Thesis writing for students
Tool and appliance rental
Tool grinding and sharpening

Jim K., an auto salesman, wanted a spare-time second income. He analyzed his sales income and found that 98 per cent of his auto sales were made after 7:00 P.M. With this fact in mind he decided to develop a second-income business he could run during the morning or afternoon hours from his home.

He came to me for advice and I showed him a master list of spare-time businesses I developed. Jim was disinterested until his eye spotted *Electrolysis for hair removal.* "That reminds me," Jim said, "I read about a new wax method for hair removal in yesterday's paper." Jim checked his local area. The wax method was not being used. He took a quick course in hair removal. Then he inserted this ad in the local paper:

> HAIR REMOVAL using the newest wax method.
> By appointment only, in your home. For free
> demonstration by trained specialist call FX-8-8800.

Soon Jim had many calls for his services. By performing his work in the client's home he had few expenses other than transportation, advertising, and supplies. Today Jim has a lucrative spare-time second-income business which he conducts at the time and on the days of his choice.

If you enjoy writing, consider one of the many activities using paper and words. Thus, the writing of publicity releases, articles, books, stories, and newspaper columns requires little investment beyond a typewriter (about $100), some paper (less than $10), and your time. Donald I. Rogers, well-known author of a business column for the *New York*

Herald Tribune, writes books in his spare time, has published five. The author of the book you are reading now, while not so well known as Mr. Rogers, has published eight books in his spare time. The royalty income from these books has provided many advantages in my personal life.

You can't write for publication? Then try writing your own newsletter about a subject you know well—your own business, hobby, or sport. How about setting up an association, club, or meeting place for members of your hobby? Trade and hobby magazines will give you free space to announce the formation of your group. Dues paid by members will reimburse you for your efforts. A young friend of mine, Peter Bruce Walton, formed Heraldry of the Air, an association specializing in aircraft insignia and markings, while still in college. He now has members throughout the United States and in foreign countries. To keep his members up to date on aircraft insignia he issues a newsletter.

SPECIALTY MANUFACTURING IS LUCRATIVE

Specialty products can bring you big spare-time profits because you have little or no competition, and the public must come to you for the product. A specialty product is one you develop yourself, or promote yourself, to serve a specific need. Typical specialty products include initial markers for golf balls, custom-made coats-of-arms, hand-made luggage for executives, personalized auto license plates containing the owner's initials or other characteristic markings, made-to-order ski suits, leatherbound editions of books, and similar items manufactured to fill the special needs or tastes of one or more individuals.

When manufacturing and selling a specialty product you deal, in general, with responsible and moneyed individuals who are willing to pay an adequate price for a well-made item. Your business is not bothered with petty bickerings or price haggling.

How can *you* get into specialty manufacturing? There are several ways. One of the simplest is to convert a hobby into a specialty. Roger K., a New York shipyard owner, built model ships as a hobby. These models weren't toys, they were exact, scale replicas built from the original shipyard drawings. As a token of appreciation to a naval friend, Roger built a model of an early iron cruiser. His friend was so delighted with the model that he sent it to the Navy Department for their study. Naval officials studied the model. It was such an excellent replica that they asked

Roger to build another model of an early ironclad battleship. Today Roger has a steady flow of work from government agencies and shipyards for his specialty product—ship models.

Many specialty products involve handwork—whittling, leatherwork, jewelry manufacture, weaving, bookbinding, bead stringing, or knitting. Develop your skill in an area of handwork and you will have an excellent chance of manufacturing a specialty product.

Perhaps you aren't a skilled hand worker. How can you get into the specialty-product business? Start by finding people who want a specialty made. Then find skilled craftsmen to manufacture the product. Here you serve as a middleman, deriving a profit for bringing the buyer and seller together.

How should you price a specialty product? There is only one answer —HIGH. By their nature, specialized products sell in small numbers because fewer people want or need them. In this case, unless you play the numbers game of wealth (Chapter 7) your chances of making a satisfactory second-income spare-time profit aren't too good.

Whenever I advise anyone on spare-time specialty manufacturing I recommend that they seek a product which promises to produce at least $50,000 income in five years. With this dollar goal in view I have the spare-time businessman analyze his market. If he believes he can sell 1,000 products in five years, then he prices each item at $50 *plus* his manufacturing costs, advertising, and sales costs. In this way he derives a gross income of $50,000 if he sells 1,000 products. Several businessmen who followed my advice and priced their specialty products this way now have an excellent spare-time income.

Specialty manufacturing of unusual products, from antiques to zebra rugs, can bring you a profitable spare-time second income. What's more, your business judgment and creativity will improve as you find and develop new products. Dealing with the customers for your products will give you new skills in handling people. Why? Because the customers for specialty products are a unique breed. As such, they will demand service and attention far beyond that of any other client you've ever met. But these unique customers are usually willing to pay your price. This means that if you find enough customers and price your product right you will earn an unusually high profit on a relatively small volume of sales.

Remember: never be afraid to price your specialty product *high*. If necessary, you can easily reduce the price to make a sale, but increasing the price once it has been set is both difficult and painful. Thus, an engineer friend of mine invented an automatic chicken feeder. He built and sold this specialty product for a while until he saw that he'd either have to give up his engineering job and concentrate on the feeder or sell out. He decided to sell the patent for $10,000. Today he often wonders if he should have asked a higher price, or if he should have raised his asking price after the first offer was made. But he recognizes that $10,000 was a good price and that if he raised it he might still have that chicken feeder for sale.

STOCK AND BOND PROFITS ON LITTLE CAPITAL

Many spare-time fortune builders turn to the stock, bond, and commodity markets to build a second income. Talk to these wealth builders and you'll find they like these markets because stocks and bonds require no maintenance, such as a building; stocks and bonds are easily moved from one locality to another at little cost; you needn't hire a superintendent or repair crew to care for stock certificates; stock and bond prices are published every weekday—you needn't wait to find an interested buyer to obtain an offering price; and, finally, stocks listed on the larger exchanges—New York, American, National, and others—have quick marketability. You can sell your securities within hours after leaving the certificates with a broker. With real estate, specialty products, and personal services you may have to wait months before you can sell an item. Let's make a brief survey of the stock, money, and commodity markets and see how you can build a spare-time second income in them.

Stock market. To expand your capital open a *margin account* with a reputable broker. With a margin account you usually pay 50 to 70 percent of the list price of a stock in cash. Thus, with 50 percent margin you would pay only $500 cash for $1000 worth of stock—say, 10 shares at $100 each. Your broker lends you the balance ($500) and pays it, along with your $500, to the seller of the stock. You are charged interest for the $500 lent you. When you sell the stock the broker deducts his $500 from the sales price.

There is no formula for "beating" the market; that is, making a profit from every stock investment. However, I have had a long investing career and can honestly say that I have never sold a stock for less than I paid for it. Thus, I have made a profit on every stock transaction during my investing career. Some of these profits were very small—only $10—but *I have never lost a dollar in the stock market*. How have I always managed to show a profit? By following these ten rules, which I developed over a number of years. Try these rules; they may work as well for you as they have for me.

(1) Buy only listed stocks. (I prefer stocks on the New York and American exchange.) (2) Do not buy a stock on the basis of a "hot" tip, rumor, or telephone call from a stranger. (3) Steer clear of new, unproven companies *unless* you are an officer of the firm and know exactly what is going on. (4) Read the financial pages of a good newspaper— *New York Times, Wall Street Journal*, every day for a year before investing in the stock market. (5) Regularly read a good business magazine—*Business Week, Fortune, Forbes, Barron's, Financial World*. (6) Select a broker having good research facilities, a broker who can give you complete details about a company in which you are interested. (7) Keep an eye on companies with which you are familiar because of your regular job. Thus, in my job I visit many electronics companies. Therefore I watch the stocks of those companies that impress me as being good investments. (8) After six months of regular reading of the financial section of your newspaper, choose eight stocks in which you'd like to invest. Select these stocks to give you diversification—that is, an interest in eight different industries. Thus, you might choose a basic metal (steel, aluminum, copper), data processing, electronics, power generation, automobiles, leisure (boats, bowling, sporting goods), aerospace, and retail stores. (9) Imagine that you've invested *your* money in these stocks. Follow each stock, every day. Don't look for a magic formula—instead, *choose those stocks promising the greatest growth,* for if a company grows, so will the worth of your stocks. (10) When you think you've learned enough about the market, invest your capital. If you choose your stocks carefully, you have an excellent chance of making a good profit in your spare time with relatively little expenditure of energy.

Don't be an in-and-out trader if you're new to the stock market. Buy the securities of modern, progressive companies and watch them grow. There are "little people" throughout our land—teachers, farmers, mechanics, restaurant workers—who have built fortunes exceeding a million dollars by starting with $3,000 to $5,000 invested in top-rated listed stocks and holding these stocks for 15 to 20 years. You too can build a fortune in your spare time if you invest wisely and if you are patient.

People will tell you about *special situations*, cases where a company is undergoing a change which will benefit its stockholders. You can make money in special situations if you study companies carefully and keep up to date on business developments. Here are eight situations which have proven profitable to me and may also earn money for you.

1. *Stock-split candidates*, that is companies about to distribute free shares of stock to their present stockholders, can build your second income. Why? When a stock splits more people "want in" because the shares are usually at a lower price and the company's earnings are often rising. If you buy before the split you will have more shares after the split (possibly 2, 3, or 4 for 1) and the price of each share may eventually rise higher than it was before the split. I have watched many stock splits and have observed that if you buy far enough in advance of the split (usually several months), and follow the ten rules given above, that you will almost always show an excellent profit. To spot potential stock-split candidates, keep a careful eye on the business news. A stock on its way to a split will gradually rise in price to a new high. Often, this high will far exceed any previous top in the stock's history. Thus, a stock whose previous high never exceeded $50 per share may inch up to $115 per share before a 2- or 3-for-1 split. The time to buy, of course, is when the stock is in the fifties. But you won't go wrong if you buy at $60, $70, or even $90. So, be alert for the stock split. Combined with margin it can quickly put a Cadillac in your garage.

2. *Merger candidates* can also put money into your pocket. Usually, a larger company buys a smaller company and merges the activities of the two. Prior to the merger the stock of the smaller company will rise in value. If you hold this stock you can sell it at a profit after it has risen to a new high, or hold the stock and become a shareholder in the larger company after the merger when your stock, generally, will have a higher value.

How do you find merger candidates? Read the financial pages of your newspaper every day. Watch for short items announcing merger discussions and agreements. My experience with mergers shows that more mergers involving a large company and a small company are successful than deals where two large companies try to merge. This, of course, is not a fixed rule. However, I have noticed that when two large companies try to merge many problems arise. With a large and small company the deal usually goes through.

If you think that merger plans you read about will go through, consider buying stock in the smaller company, if the merger will produce a growth-oriented firm. In general, the money you have invested in a small company grows more when merged with a large company. Also, the stock of a smaller company is likely to be lower priced and nearer its true value than the stock of a larger company. In merger situations in which you buy small-company stock you will often find the stock is unlisted—that is, sold over-the-counter. This is one situation in which I recommend that you buy, if necessary, an unlisted security. To learn the typical steps in a merger, follow one from start to finish in your paper. Pay particular attention to the stock prices of both companies *before* and *after* the merger. Then you will know what to expect when you buy stock in a merger candidate.

3. *Prospective exchange listing* can send stock prices soaring. Thus, a price runup frequently occurs when an over-the-counter (OTC) stock applies for listing on one of the big exchanges—American, New York, National. Thus, an OTC stock priced at $22.75 jumped to $44.00 within three weeks from the time its listing on a big exchange was announced. Another jumped from $6.63 to $9.12 in about four weeks. A third jumped from $9.00 to $14.75 in about four weeks. Some of these stocks later dropped to their OTC levels. But if you bought when the application for listing was announced, or shortly thereafter, you could have made an excellent profit by selling at, or near, the high.

Two-thirds of the newly listed stocks I've watched decline after being listed on one of the big exchanges. This decline, however, doesn't begin until several days or weeks after the listing, so you have plenty of time to sell at a good profit, if your stock rises after being listed (as most do). Also, most of the listed stocks eventually rise and exceed their previous highs in a bull market.

4. *Stock rights* can often be profitable investments because they can offer good price variation and better-than-current margin requirements. For example, a well-known stock made rights available for purchase of its stock at $100 per share when the market price was $148.50 per share. You had to have 20 rights to buy one share at $100. The rights cost about $2.375 each, or $47.50 for 20. Thus, to buy one share of this blue-chip stock at $100 you would put up only $47.50 (= 20 $\times$ $2.375). When the closing date on the rights arrives (usually about two months after first being offered) you can borrow from your broker, if you have a

margin account, the $100 per share to buy the stock. If you bought a share of the same stock without using the rights you would have to put up about $104 (= 0.70 $\times$ $148.50) if the margin requirement was 70 per cent. The $47.50 cash you paid for 20 rights is only 32 per cent of the $148.50 market price. Thus, with $1500 to invest you could obtain about 31 shares by using rights, but only 14 shares by using 70 per cent margin. Also, since the rights price can vary, you may be able to buy at a slightly lower price if you carefully follow the rights price.

Rights increase your leverage, giving you more shares to profit from, if the stock price rises. The rights may also permit you to obtain shares at a price well below the current market price. When purchasing rights I usually wait until about half the "exercise period" has elapsed. Study of several rights offerings shows that rights prices may decline, reaching their low at about the midpoint of the offering period—four weeks in an eight-week offering period. Then the rights price usually rises until the offer closes.

Should you prefer to speculate in rights only, you can make a neat profit, if the price of the stock rises. Just be sure to either sell the rights or exercise (use) them before the allotted time runs out. If you do not take either action, you will lose the money invested in the rights.

5. *A broker's advice can be excellent.* Many brokers provide free research and investment advice to their clients. One broker recommends about 10 stocks for purchase each year. In 11 of the last 14 years the recommended stocks outperformed the market averages (Dow-Jones, Standard & Poor's). This broker provides his recommendations free to anyone requesting them. In 14 years a $10,000 investment in the recommended stocks, adjusted each year for the new recommendations, would have grown to $124,190. Such a record, while not a guarantee of future performance, is very encouraging to the spare-time second-income fortune builder.

Many brokerage houses offer excellent free advice. By combining such recommendations with my own studies of companies, and the stock market, I have *always* been able to show a profit on *every* stock investment. Study the broker ads in your newspaper and send for the free material offered. Study it carefully; then choose a broker. If you choose wisely your fortune will grow steadily and surely. This is a grand feeling.

Much observation and study leads me to believe that, for me at least, advice and research from brokers is more useful than so-called stock-market letters. Friends of mine who read market letters never seem satisfied with the advice in one letter, so they subscribe to two, then three. A good broker can give you excellent advice at no charge. Try it and see. For excellent advice on making unusual profits in the stock market read *Fundamentals for Profit in Undervalued Stocks*, Prentice-Hall, 1964.

6. *Convertible bonds* allow you to play many of your favorite stocks with little cash. You need put up only 15 to 35 per cent cash (margin) to buy a convertible bond. This is much less cash than the 50 to 70 per cent margin required for common stocks.

A convertible bond or debenture is like any other corporate bond except that it can be converted, i.e., exchanged, for a certain number of shares of common stock of a company at a specific price called the conversion price. A date for the conversion may also be specified; thus you may be allowed 10 years from the time of purchase during which you may convert the bond to stock. If you do not convert, you still own the bond and can expect to collect regular interest income as well as the face value of the bond at maturity.

What are the advantages of convertible bonds? There are two: (a) You need less cash to purchase this type of bond. (b) In a rising market you can often convert your bond into stock at a much lower price than the current market value of the stock. You can sell the conversion privilege, or convert and sell the stock. In a declining market a convertible bond usually will not fall as much in value as the common stock of the same company. Thus, you are protected by the face value of the bond against large losses.

Wise use of convertible bonds can build your fortune with minimum risk. Seth Glickenhaus and Lawrence Lembo speculated in convertible bonds of one of America's largest blue-chip companies. These wise investors made $8 million from their investment. Mr. Lembo retired at the age of fifty-seven. Mr. Glickenhaus, forty-five, returned to college but later came back to Wall Street.

If convertible bonds interest you, ask your broker for full information about investing in them. You may find that these bonds will build your second-income fortune with minimum effort and low capital.

7. *U.S. Government bonds*, like corporate bonds, can build your spare-time fortune, if you invest wisely. Government bonds have several advantages: (a) They are easy to sell when you need money. (b) Broker-

age fees are lower than for many corporate stocks and bonds. (c) Required margin is low—often 5 per cent or less. While you *can* lose money in U.S. Government bonds, you can also show good profits. Though some people hesitate about speculating in U.S. Government bonds, many other people take a different view. "Someone," they say, "has to buy these bonds. Is it a crime that the securities increase in value? It certainly isn't."

You can buy government bonds through your broker or bank. Treasury bills are auctioned every Monday by Federal Reserve Banks. If you wait for an opportune moment you can buy these bonds at a favorable discount. You can obtain details about other U.S. Government bonds from your broker or bank. In general, you have a greater chance of building a sizeable second-income spare-time fortune through U.S. Government bonds than through the municipal bonds offered by various cities and towns throughout the country. Keep one fact in mind when buying any bond—your margin requirements will be much lower if you work through your bank.

8. *No-load mutual funds* can, in a rising market, help you avoid any commissions on share purchases and sales. Today there are about forty such funds. Many of these have excellent records. For details of these records, refer to *Trusts & Estates* magazine or Johnson's *Investment Company Charts*. These two references will show you which funds did best in various market conditions.

When you speculate in a no-load mutual fund you must keep a careful watch on both general market conditions and on the share value of the fund. For the share value will rise and fall with the level of the market. To earn the greatest profit from no-load speculation buy when share values are low and sell when they are high. These values generally correspond to low and high values of the stock market. Thus, in 1962 one no-load fund was selling for $17 per share. A year and a half later this same share was worth almost $25. You would have a capital gain of $8 per share in this time, plus the dividends that were paid. Most no-load funds are identified in the daily mutual-fund tables by having their price quoted at "net asset value."

FOREIGN EXCHANGE—BONANZA FOR TRAVEL ENTHUSIASTS

If you have a mathematical-type of mind you can speculate in foreign exchange. Your broker or bank will be glad to cooperate with you and might even offer some free advice. Some banks may be willing to take your foreign exchange business without any cash down—i.e., no margin. Others ask for a small down payment of from 1 to 10 per cent when you deal in relatively stable currency. If the currency fluctuates rapidly, you may have to put up as much as 50 per cent in cash.

When speculating in foreign exchange you agree to buy or sell a certain number of marks, francs, guilders, or other currency, at a future date. You hope, if you buy, that the exchange rate will rise and you can sell at a profit. Thus, suppose you buy German marks at 24 cents each and hold them until the price rises to 25 cents. Your profit is one cent per mark. This may seem small, but when you need no cash, or very little, you can buy enough marks to earn a generous profit. If you bought $30,000 worth of currency in a transaction with $1,000 down for delivery in 60 days and the value of the currency rose 5 per cent (not an unusual rise) you would have a profit of 0.05 ($30,000) = $1,500 in 60 days on an investment of only $1,000. You would, of course, also recover your $1,000 investment.

Study the financial pages of your newspaper to learn the latest exchange rates. If you travel widely, your knowledge of exchange rates and world conditions will help you make more profitable investments. What's more, you can't lose much in foreign exchange speculation except in times of grave emergencies in the political situation in the world. By keeping up to date on world affairs you can anticipate, to a certain degree, when political upheavals may occur.

Another advantage of foreign-exchange speculation is its simplicity. All you need do is phone your order (called a contract) to your bank or broker. The deal is completed through the mail when you send and receive checks. This arrangement is ideal for the spare-time second-income fortune builder—particularly if you're working on several different businesses at once. After you've acquired some experience, you'll try three-way purchases—say francs with dollars, marks with francs, and dollars with marks. If you invest wisely, such purchases can be highly profitable, possibly $250 profit on a $1,000 investment, all within a few days.

COMMODITY FUTURES—LOW-MARGIN INVESTMENTS

Commodity futures—the buying of wheat, soybeans, wool, barley, cocoa, and similar products for delivery at a future date—require little margin. You can get by with as little as 5 to 15 per cent cash. Elliot Spring, while part owner of an electronics laboratory, built an initial investment of $10,000 to over $300,000 in less than a year in soybeans. To achieve such an increase in his investment he devoted many hours to study and analysis of the market.

When you buy a commodity contract today it will usually run from three to six months. Thus, if you buy a contract for several thousand bushels of corn at $1.130 per bushel and the price rises to $1.430 per bushel by the end of your contract you'll have a gross profit of $1.430 − 1.130 = $0.30 per bushel. Once again—low margin can bring you big profits. For a good discussion of commodity futures see Robert Gardner's fine *How to Make Money in the Commodity Market*, Prentice-Hall, and *How to Read and Understand Financial and Business News*, by the Financial and Business News Staff of *The New York Times*, published by Doubleday & Company, Inc. Mr. Gardner tells of an electrician who invested $5,700 in soybean futures; one hour later he had a $1,200 profit. A real-estate man invested $4,800 and was $1,200 richer in 2½ hours. A professional commodity trader made $150,000 in 19 trading days.

FOREIGN STOCKS AND COMPANIES CAN PAY BIG PROFITS

The American dollar is respected and highly valued throughout the world. What's better, your dollar will buy more overseas. For example you can have a ship or boat built in Japan for about 40 per cent of its United States price. There are three types of foreign investments you should investigate in your search for a spare-time second-income fortune. These are: (1) foreign stocks, (2) overseas firms, and (3) investment in foreign ventures. Let's examine each one briefly.

(1) *Foreign stocks* can bring big returns if you are familiar with the companies, customs, and language of a country. Then you can research the better companies and choose one or more to invest in. If you aren't familiar with a country and its language you should wait until you visit it before investing. With some on-the-spot experience you will be better equipped for wise investment.

There are a number of foreign stock exchanges whose offerings you'll want to scan. These exchanges include London, England; Frankfurt, West Germany; Milan, Italy; Paris, France; Tokyo, Japan; Zurich, Switzerland; Amsterdam, Holland; and Sydney, Australia. The Tokyo exchange offers thousands of low-priced stocks and is characterized, at times, by enormous rises and falls in price. If you want action the Tokyo exchange will give it.

Your safest bets in foreign stocks are solid industries such as steel, petroleum, electronics, data processing, automobiles or mining. Buy the blue-chips in these and similar industries and your investments will be safe. Your stocks, if chosen wisely, may grow faster than if invested in similar firms in the United States. Avoid, in your second-income fortune search, the penny mineral stocks, the virgin oil claims, and similar wild schemes. You have little chance of showing a profit and you may lose all the savings you invest. The great distance you are from the actual site, the differences in language and business customs, can be a major disadvantage. Mark Twain, the famous author of *The Adventures of Huckleberry Finn*, lost several hundred thousand dollars investing in a number of promotions outside the writing field. These promotions included a spiral hat pin and a steam pulley. Unwise speculation can lead you to lose many dollars, particularly in areas with which you are unfamiliar.

There are two steps you can take to protect your investment in foreign stocks. First, you can buy shares of a mutual fund which invests in foreign stocks. The managers of these funds have a wide knowledge of the stocks in which they invest and they seldom choose unwisely. In addition, you can buy foreign stocks listed on exchanges in the United States. Your broker can assist in your choice of worthwhile stocks. Many foreign stocks listed on exchanges in the United States offer excellent growth opportunities.

(2) *Foreign firms* can often be bought for little money. Thus, an electronics firm in Kofu City, Japan has about 100 employees and a capital of less than $1,500. Another electronics firm in Kyoto, Japan, has 10 employees and a capital of less than $3,000. Either of these firms might be purchased for a small amount of money—certainly less than $10,000. If you can't afford this much, consider purchasing a one-half or one-quarter interest.

In some overseas countries you may have to leave your profits in the country in which the firm is located. This isn't a serious problem; all you need do is visit the country in which your firm is located and spend your profits there. You might even be able to have your profits deposited in an overseas bank and then *borrow* from that bank against your overseas fare. Of course, if you travel overseas to conduct business on which you pay income taxes to the United States, you have an excellent chance of deducting, on your tax return, these expenses as legitimate "ordinary and necessary" costs of doing business.

If you enjoy travel, an overseas firm may be the best answer to your spare-time second-income fortune search, for it combines travel with profit. What could be more attractive to travel-minded men and women?

Where profit is your only motive, investing in a foreign firm might prove more troublesome than it's worth. To enjoy your profits from a foreign firm you must be interested in activities outside the United States. Also, a knowledge of overseas business practices is necessary, though you can learn this by some study of the many excellent books available on the subject.

(3) *Investment in foreign ventures* is often more profitable, from a time and effort standpoint, than buying an overseas firm. To invest in a foreign venture all you need do is supply some capital—after you've found a worthwhile project. A good friend of mine, Dan K., wanted to invest some money in a foreign venture. He came to me for advice. Since he was interested in airplanes and flying, I suggested that he make friends with some airline pilots from the country he was interested in. He did just this, by calling one of the big airlines to learn what hotel the pilots stayed at during their layovers in the United States. He spent some time in the lobby of the hotel and soon made friends with several pilots.

Talks with the pilots showed that some were interested in opening a flying school in the area of their home base. Dan K. invested $3,000 in the school. Today he collects $4,500 per year from this investment because the school is highly successful. Once a year he visits the school to check on its condition. Between visits his pilot friends keep him informed by telephoning him during their layovers in the United States. These pilots also serve as instructors in the school, thereby increasing their spare-time income.

There are many other ways to learn of good opportunities for foreign investment. Study copies of big-city newspapers—London, Paris, Rome, Tokyo, Sydney. You'll see many Capital Wanted ads in these papers. Trade journals, business magazines, and trade association bulletins are excellent sources of leads about ventures requiring capital. You can check the authenticity of a proposal by studying the facts supplied you. Further information may be available at the nearest consular office of the country in which the business is located. Local trade representatives in seacoast cities may also be able to provide useful facts and background data.

There are many countries in which you can invest profitably in your spare time. In Western Europe these include—England, France, West Germany, Denmark, Sweden, Finland, Holland, Belgium, Italy, Spain, Portugal; in the Far East, Japan, Nationalist China, the Philippines; Australia; in South America, Venezuela, Brazil, Argentina, Chile, Colombia; Central America and Mexico. Choose the country or area and then seek the facts.

Fortunes can be made in overseas ventures if you choose wisely. Pick a spare-time business that interests you and your chances for success are good.

LOW-CAPITAL INVESTMENTS DO PAY OFF

You really don't need much money to go into a profitable spare-time business if you can devote time and energy to your project. Bud Friedman started a highly successful coffee house, The Improvisation, in Manhattan for $220. His furnishings are clean and attractive. Young actors and people with an interest in the theatre patronize this well-run coffee house. If they feel the urge to perform they can do so, if Bud approves.

So look around your local area today. There *is* a need you can fill in your spare time. Fill this need with a low-capital modest-time venture and you will soon be on the road towards a spare-time second-income fortune.

The spare-time second-income ventures you learned about in Chapter 9 are fine when you have only a small amount of capital. With more capital—say $5,000 to $10,000, or more—you can invest money instead of time. The larger investment allows you more time to pursue another business, or an interesting hobby. Let's see how you can release the powerful force of investment to build your wealth while you laze, doze, play, or work.

"You need money to earn money," is a remark you'll often hear. Like most

<table>
<tr><td>11</td></tr>
</table>

Earn More

in Moderate-Capital

Minimum-Time Ventures

common sayings it is partially true—here is the reasoning behind it.

If you invest a moderate amount of capital, instead of a small amount, you own more, or all, of a business. Fewer debts hang over your head. You are freer to act the way you wish. Your time is more your own. You can spend more hours with your family.

Calvin T., an accountant, invested $10,000 in a local hardware store as an "absentee owner." He hired a bright young man to operate the store. Instead of trying to pay his store manager the minimum salary possible, Calvin paid him the maximum he could afford and gave him a share of the profits. Further, Calvin promised his store manager a 1 per cent ownership in the hardware store each year the profits exceeded those of the previous year by 10 per cent. The young manager jumped at the opportunity because each time he made a sale a few pennies were credited to him.

Today Calvin T. hardly visits his hardware store. His young manager keeps the profits rolling in at an ever-rising rate. Calvin has given up some of his ownership but he feels it is well worth it because his monthly income from the store long ago repaid his initial investment. Calvin has branched out to real estate, gas stations, and other activities. His moderate investment has given him time—free hours to think about and devote to other ventures.

With moderate capital you can invest in successful businesses that require less doctoring to show a good profit. When you're just beginning to build your spare-time second-income fortune you are willing to invest large blocks of time to earn a profit. With money in your pocket you can wait for the right opportunity to increase your fortune. What's more, the profits you derive can be pyramided to build a string of lucrative ventures which deliver sizeable checks to your mailbox every month of the year.

MORTGAGE VENTURES THAT HAVE CLASS—AND PROFITS

Low-cost rental property can be profitable. High-class rental property can be even more so, and the only difference between low- and high-cost rental property is an extra investment of a few thousand dollars. Thus, the apartment house or industrial building you take over with $10,000 down can be much more lucrative and far easier to run than the no-money-down or $1,000-down building.

High-class rental property is usually newer, requires less attention, and has more desirable tenants than low-cost property. An apartment manager is easier to find and keep. Renting agents are more anxious to work with you. Evictions are seldom a problem—you'll hardly ever have to call your lawyer. So, keep an eye open for such rental properties. You'll find them listed in the sources described in Chapter 9.

Many modest-capital fortune builders avoid the problems of building rentals, maintenance, and taxes by buying second mortgages and trust deeds. These investors specialize in mortgages they can buy at a discount. Such mortgages return an interest on the investment *and* are protected by any growth in value that occurs in the property. The monthly repayments received on the mortgage are a regular, dependable income. Growth in value of the property allows you, the investor, to speculate at the same time.

Suppose you buy at a 20 per cent discount a five-year $10,000 mortgage that pays 8 per cent interest. You pay $10,000 − 0.20 ($10,000) = $8,000 for the mortgage. But your interest is figured on the undiscounted mortgage and is 0.08 ($10,000) = $800 per year. This is an actual interest rate of 10 per cent on your $8,000 investment. At the end of five years you will have received 5 ($800) interest + $2,000 discount = $6,000 gross profit on an investment of only $8,000. Your annual yield will thus be 20 per cent. This is excellent, considering that you do nothing but invest your money and then keep track of the monthly payments. The owner of the building has all the maintenance and renting responsibilities.

Many of my friends regularly get 10 per cent interest on their mortgage investments. When the discount is added, the annual yield commonly runs between 15 and 20 per cent. Check your local papers for "Mortgages Bought and Sold" ads. Then contact the broker, telling him how much you have to invest and the yield you seek. You will be delighted with the opportunities he offers you when you have a moderate amount of capital to invest.

Instead of buying a mortgage at a discount you can buy a rental property with minimum cash down. Study the property to determine how its income can be increased with minimum capital investment. Then advertise the property, clearly indicating its potential earnings. Ask for the least possible cash down—perhaps even less than your down payment —but base the sale price on the *potential* earnings of the building or property. Many investors are looking for deals where they can put a little money down and derive a large income. These investors enjoy improving a property. Eventually most of them sell out at a good profit. You can do this, if you wish, or you can concentrate on selling the property *before* you increase its income. Let's see how that works.

Suppose you bought a 20-family apartment house for $1,000 down. The sale price was $19,000, based on a stated profit of $3,000 per year. You study the building carefully and find that an investment of $1,500 can raise the annual income to $5,000. This appears to make the building worth $30,000; that is six times its annual profit. To allow some room for dickering you run this ad:

> 20-UNIT APT. HOUSE. Potential profit $5,000 per year. Price $31,000; cash $1,500. Write Box A3881.

You mentally resolve to sell at any price higher than $27,999 and any cash payment more than $999. Thus you have $3,000 ($31,000 — 28,000) in the price and $500 ($1500 — 1000) to bargain with. A buyer writes you arranging an appointment to see the property. You show it to him, or have a real estate agent show it. The prospective buyer offers you $29,000 and $750 cash. You make a counter offer of $29,500 and $1000 cash. Your offer is accepted. Let's see what you achieved.

You owe $18,000 on the property, less any reduction made in the mortgage by your monthly payments. We'll ignore this reduction, even though it would put a few extra dollars in your pocket. The buyer gives you $1000 cash and a mortgage for $28,500. You use this mortgage to pay off the $18,000 existing mortgage ($19,000 price — $1,000 cash down) and come out holding a $10,500 mortgage ($28,500 — $18,000). At 6 per cent interest with a 10-year term your monthly income from the mortgage would be about $117.00. Your only costs were advertising, closing fees, and incidentals. Thus, with only a $1,000 investment, which you recovered, you've obtained a monthly income exceeding $115. Should the buyer default on his payments you can take over the building and sell it to someone else. While the $117.00 per month brings in less than the $3,000 profit from the building, you are free of many problems—renting, maintenance, operation, clearing sidewalks of snow. Your income is free and clear, *and* you do nothing for it once the building is sold. To learn more about similar real estate deals, read the books listed in Chapter 9.

RUN LOCAL SERVICES FOR THE BEST PEOPLE IN TOWN

It's nice to work for the successful people in town. They're more interesting, have money to spend, and will buy your service if you use the right approach. Today the town pace-setters spend about 42 cents of every dollar on services. You can make part of this money yours, if you plan well.

What services can you sell the leading businessmen in town? There are many—cocktail lounges, taverns, restaurants, beauty salons, massage parlors, antiques, specialized mail order, animal care, portrait photography, art collections, insurance, sports cars, custom jewelry, special garments, wake-up call service, wall-washing, gardening, banquet catering, basement finishing, bathroom decorating, finding special books, loans, manicuring, newspaper delivery, pest extermination, and hundreds of others. Each of these is a potential for your spare-time second-income fortune. All you need in each case is a unique approach that makes your service different and more desirable than others.

To attract the wealthier people in town, your service must not only be unique in its approach, but it should also have these five characteristics: (1) modern equipment in spotless condition (if you need equipment in the business); (2) neat, clean uniforms for yourself and all other personnel; (3) attractive calling cards, billheads, stationery; (4) a prestige mailing address, if you conduct any business by mail; (5) well-prepared advertisements placed in publications read by your prospective clients or customers.

Dealing with the wealthy and near-wealthy has other advantages. If your service is unique you perform it at your convenience. Clients who have money are willing to pay high prices for good service. When wealthy people learn that you are working in your spare time to build a second-income fortune they will often give you leads on other opportunities or will refer you to their friends who may also become clients. Many beginning spare-time fortune builders got their first big break from a tip given by a wealthy client.

Cultivate the wealthy people in your town or area whenever you can. The rewards can be far greater than you might ever expect. One spare-time fortune builder I know of earns up to $500 per week walking, grooming, and training dogs for wealthy clients in New York City. On some days he will have as many as eight dogs at once on his leashes. His three main expenses are shoes (he wears out a pair every two weeks), advertising, and billheads. He enjoys his work because it is healthy and he is very fond of dogs. His business has grown so rapidly that he now has an assistant to help him.

Before beginning a business for the better people in town, make a careful study of where these people live, how many of them there are, and what spending habits they have. Thus, if your town has a large number of people who enjoy drinking but do few home repairs, your chances for success would be much greater if you opened a liquor store or home maintenance shop than if you opened a hardware store.

Specialty dress, coat, and sportswear shops can be lucrative in the right part of town. The secrets of successful shops of this type are unusual garments, high prices, a distinctive name and atmosphere for the shop, and personalized attention for each customer. You can build a profitable spare-time business in this type of shop if you enjoy working with people and care enough to give them the service and attention they desire.

Samuel Segal, inventor of the well-known Segal lock, served the affluent people in town by developing a device to protect their homes and belongings. Mr. Segal invented the lock while he held a full-time position as a New York City policeman. Later he founded his own company to manufacture the lock and other hardware. He expanded to form a safety razor company. His products are used by people throughout the world today.

Wealthy people buy and sell real estate more than people with less money. Why? Because wealthy people enjoy buying and improving farms, ranches, estates, and similar properties. When they tire of a property they sell it, usually at a good profit. You can cash in on this by becoming a real estate salesman. All you need do in most states is to attend a short course to prepare for the real estate license examination. This exam, while thorough, can be passed by any intelligent person who prepares himself properly. Once you have your license you can open a real estate agency dealing in better properties or obtain a part-time job in an agency of this type. Many of today's real estate salesmen are part-time employees who earn excellent commissions on the sale of better properties.

People of substance prefer waterfront properties, houses with a view, homes designed by well-known architects, houses with an historical past, converted homes (barns to houses and the like), large and small estates, and similar unusual real estate buys. Find such properties and you'll have little trouble building your spare-time second-income fortune. Be alert at all times to unusual homes and properties. Then when one is offered for sale you will be in a good position to act as the agent and find a buyer. Keep a list of prospective buyers and the type of homes they seek.

Local services for well-to-do people pay off. Watch your local papers for ads for services that need filling, and for establishments or properties offered for sale. A good friend of mine built a large fortune in his spare time by buying a run-down nursing home and converting it into a first-class rest home for the wealthy. Later he sold it at a high profit and pyramided the profits into baking, real estate, food, and other activities. You can do the same with cocktail lounges, taverns, restaurants, and similar businesses. All you need is some capital and a knowledge of what the prosperous people seek. Try it and watch your spare-time profits grow.

SPECIALIZED MAIL ORDER PAYS BIG PROFITS

Successful, part-time mail order operators can earn as much as $25,000 per year working out of their homes. Thus, some schoolteachers earn $20,000 per year operating a mail order business after school hours. A few part-time mail order operators earn $40,000 to $50,000 per year but your chances of reaching this income level aren't too great unless you are extremely lucky.

Before going into mail order choose the type of product line you wish to handle—*general* or *specialized*. In a general line you might sell everything from acorns to zippers. There are a number of mail order franchise firms that can help you get started by supplying catalogs with your name printed on them. You mail the catalogs to lists you choose. When orders come in you have the mail order firm ship the merchandise, keeping the difference between the catalog list price and the wholesale price. Refer to men's magazines for ads of mail order firms interested in granting new franchises.

In specialty mail order you sell a line of related products such as smoker's supplies, auto parts, or electronic kits. Specialty mail order selling is best for those spare-time fortune builders who have a wide knowledge of a certain field, or a deep interest in a hobby. Chapter 12 gives several examples of how hobbyists have converted their interest into a lucrative spare-time business.

Studies of a number of mail order operators show that the most successful general-line sellers are men who have a strong business background. Specialty-line operators are usually people who have narrower training—engineers, accountants, machinists. Use this general guide when planning your spare-time mail order career. There's money to be earned in either line. In a recent year $28 billion of goods and services were sold by mail order in the United States.

What are good lines for mail order beginners? There are many—books for specialized groups like investors, businessmen, lawyers; tools for tradesmen, mechanics, hobbyists; vitamins for health and strength; special foods for health faddists; antique furniture, guns, tools; used correspondence courses; hot-rod auto parts; land and acreage; and many others. Choose a line like one of these if you have a knowledge of the products and the potential customers for them. Otherwise, obtain a franchise from a general mail order firm and begin making mailings.

Mail order can give you an excellent return for your investment. You should have at least $1,000 to start, preferably $2,000 or more. With this much invested in products and mailing lists you are sure to succeed if you make test mailings and run test ads before going all out and mailing several thousand circulars. To earn the highest return on your investment, get several books on mail order from your local library. Study these carefully. An excellent book for beginners is A. C. Chapman's *Mail Order Program*. Mr. Chapman borrowed $32 to start his mail order business, and within a few months was averaging more than $2,000 per month. His income ranged to as high as $15,000 per month. Two other fine books by experienced mail order operators are *How I Made $1,000,000 in Mail Order*, E. Joseph Cossman, Prentice-Hall, Inc., and Irwin Graham's *How to Sell Through Mail Order*, McGraw-Hill Book Company.

START YOUR OWN MUTUAL FUND WITH MODERATE CAPITAL

When thinking of mutual funds most people envision millions of dollars invested by thousands of stockholders. This is an accurate picture of *large* mutual funds. Yet a mutual fund need not be large to be successful. There are many *small* mutual funds today, and some out-perform the large funds.

What do you need to begin a mutual fund? Two items: an investing concept, and at least $10,000 cash. Let's see how you can turn these into a profitable fund.

Most mutual funds aim at protecting the investor's capital while providing at least one other attraction. This may be growth of the invested capital (i.e., a growth fund), high income from the invested capital (i.e., an income fund), or investment in a specific industry, such as electronics, chemicals, aircraft, or missiles and space. The fund is advertised and sold to investors on the basis of its investment concept—protection and growth, protection and income, protection and shares in electronics firms, and so forth. Since the most desirable investment concepts were selected by mutual funds founded long ago, you must seek a concept that is unique. You can develop such a concept if your past experience is different from that of most people.

Look to your own interests to find a unique concept. Thus, experience and interest in banking might lead you to form a fund specializing in bank stocks. Other experience might lead you to choose ocean transportation, airlines, or trucking firms. Seek a growth industry that appeals to as large a group of investors as possible. Choose an industry in which you have friends. As a seaman or ship's officer you might pick ocean transportation and concentrate on selling shares of the fund to your shipmates. Instead of one industry you might choose several that incorporate an investing concept like growth through population expansion; scientific developments for future progress; or health aids for the ill.

Recently two young research men in the office of a California stock broker had a unique concept for a mutual fund. They bought a sick "income" fund and switched it to convertible bonds and stocks. This unique concept turned a share loss to a share gain. In less than a year the number of shareholders increased from about 700 to more than 1,000. Today the fund continues its healthy growth because shareholders are convinced its unique concept is profitable.

Make a "dry run" of your fund for at least a year before investing money in it. Select your stocks or bonds and record the choices in a notebook. Keep an accurate record of brokerage fees, dividends received, and capital gains resulting from the sale of securities. Project these costs and gains for larger purchases—five, ten, and twenty times your theoretical investment. If your transactions show a profit you are ready to consider founding a fund. Ideally, you should have three to five years of experience with "dry runs" before starting the fund, but most people are unwilling to wait this long unless they have another spare-time business that is earning a profit.

Obtain offering circulars from several mutual funds once you have decided to form your own fund. Study these circulars and pattern yours after them. You'll need some legal advice and some associates to make the fund conform to various legal requirements, but neither item is a major problem.

Your profits from the fund can come from two sources: management fees, and increases in share value. Management fees are legitimate sums paid a fund manager for selecting, buying, and selling shares held in the fund's portfolio. This fee varies with the size of the fund; for allowable rates consult the latest SEC recommendations. The fee, however, is entirely adequate to repay you for the time you expend managing the fund. Share-value increases will also provide income to you, if you invest some of your own money in the mutual fund. Since you must buy a few stocks or bonds to start the fund, your chances for profits over those provided by the management fee are good, if you pick the right securities.

You *can* run a profitable and interesting mutual fund. All you need is an investing concept and moderate capital. So get out your notebook today and pick the securities that fit your concept. Even if you don't start the fund you will gain some useful "dry run" investing experience. You can always use this experience to guide your own part-time second-income stock market investments.

TRY THE WORLD OF BOOKS FOR SOPHISTICATED PROFITS

Paper and words can, as we saw in Chapter 9, be built into a lucrative business with hardly any capital. With moderate capital you can build a profitable business in the world of books. With little capital, you usually must write books or articles to make up for the missing dollars. With moderate capital you need not write; instead you buy and sell, or manufacture and sell. Let's look at each.

Book lovers throughout the world have special interests in first editions, out-of-print volumes, books on specialized subjects, anniversary volumes, autographed copies, original manuscripts, and similar items. These book lovers will pay high prices for the items they want. A friend of mine once paid $5 for a rare first edition and sold it the next day to a client for $1,500. That's a 30,000 per cent profit in one day! How does anyone rate such a profit? *By knowing his product and his market.*

To get started in book selling and buying take these six steps: (1) Explore the market for books of various types—first editions, out-of-print works, and other rarities. (2) Decide which type will return you the highest profit. (3) Investigate the potential supply of such books in local auctions of home furnishings, estate sales, library sales, and similar offerings of property. (4) Estimate what your average investment per volume will be. Some booksellers will buy an entire library just to get one copy of a valuable book. (5) Compare your average cost with the probable average sales price. Your gross profit should be at least 300 per cent before deducting overhead costs—rent, light, heat, advertising, postage, telephone, travel. (6) Invest a small sum if you have a potential gross profit of 300 per cent or higher. If you make the sale and show a profit, invest some more money. Soon you'll have a lucrative spare-time second income.

Most specialty booksellers I know specialize in one or a few types of books. They issue typewritten catalogs at irregular intervals, sending copies to a mailing list built from small ads in literary papers and magazines. Over a period of time they build a list of regular customers who buy their books. Almost every small specialty bookseller operates from his home—the attic, basement, even the kitchen. Since book lovers are accustomed to buying by mail there is no need for a store or warehouse.

If specialty bookselling interests you from a profit standpoint, take the six steps outlined above. Also, get copies of the mail order books listed earlier in this chapter. After a few months as a spare-time second-income bookseller you may even become a book collector, like your customers; but even the most ardent collectors are bitten by the profit bug. Then they sell their favorite items—usually at a profit, because with specialty books time is always working in your favor.

Book manufacturing and selling is another profitable spare-time business worth your investigation. Instead of seeking unusual books, you manufacture them. Thus, Henry Chafetz and Sidney Solomon, bookseller owners of Cooper Square Publishers, Inc., published a 996-copy two-volume edition of the Gutenberg Bible, originally published in 1455. At the time of publication there were only 14 copies of the original Gutenberg in the United States. One copy had sold for $511,000 at a European auction. The Chafetz and Solomon replica edition sells for $750 for the two-volume set. Applying the number principles of business to this project you can see that the total income generated from the sale of 996 copies will be close to $750,000. This is more than double the $300,000 investment these businessmen made in the manufacture of the book.

In a similar manner the same firm published the complete Library of Congress Catalog in 167 volumes. The list price was $1,500 per set.

Where can *you* find books to publish and what will your costs be? There are two prime sources of suitable books for the spare-time publisher: out-of-print works, and manuscripts submitted by experienced and aspiring authors.

Out-of-print works are those books other publishers no longer print because sale of the title is too small. For certain of these books there is, however, a steady and continuing market. Thus, Peter Smith, of Gloucester, Mass., regularly sells a variety of out-of-print books to libraries, schools, and similar markets. Eugene Rachlis, a successful author of books in his own right, is a partner in Octagon Books, a firm which reprints scholarly works which have gone out of print.

Another source of books is from amongst works that are in the public domain, that is, not protected by copyright. Such books include American works copyrighted more than 56 years ago on which a new copyright has not been obtained, and many books issued by State and Federal governments.

To obtain manuscripts from experienced and aspiring authors all you need do is submit your needs to any of several writer's magazines. You will be flooded with manuscripts. Among these you may find some suitable ones. You can also send notices of your needs to literary agents listed in the New York, Chicago, Los Angeles, and San Francisco telephone books, or in *Literary Market Place*.

Once you have a suitable manuscript you must choose a low-cost production method. Take the material to several reputable printers and ask them for cost estimates. Conferring with several printers will give you a quick course in the elements of book manufacture.

You'll have to invest at least $3,000 to manufacture 1,000 copies of a 200–300 page cloth-bound book. The actual investment depends on the subject matter, number of illustrations, type of paper and binding. To recover twice your investment the net income per copy must be at least $6. For this reason your safest bet in spare-time book publishing is nonfiction. People are willing to pay higher prices for nonfiction than for novels, poetry, and similar works.

Once you publish a book you have the task of selling it to recover your investment. This is a specialized task which you might consider giving to a sales representative if selling doesn't interest you. Or, if you wish, you can sell the book yourself. There are several popular methods of selling books—mail order, bookstores, overseas. Your best sources of information on book sales procedures are other books such as *What Happens in Book Publishing*, edited by C. B. Grannis, Columbia University Press, which is an excellent source of information. This book lists a number of other valuable references you will find helpful in your work.

TWENTY OTHER PROFITABLE, MODERATE-CAPITAL VENTURES

There are hundreds of other moderate-capital ventures in which you can earn excellent spare-time profits. Here are twenty worth your study. Each is in capsule form so you can quickly determine your interest in it. Typical starting-capital needs are given.

1. THEATRICAL PRODUCTIONS, often called "off-Broadway" because the shows run in low-rent non-theatre districts, can be lucrative. Production costs are low because you use amateur, or near-amateur actors, little scenery, a cheap theatre. "Angels" (interested backers) are easy to find and they are usually willing to put up $500 to $5,000 for a percentage of the profits. Steer clear of theatrical productions unless you like the theatre, plays, and acting. Since all your help is part-time and most performances run in the evening, this is an ideal spare-time second-income source. *Minimum starting capital: $5,000*

2. ANTIQUE GUNS are booming in interest and sales. Promote your wares with ads in gun magazines. The most popular items are Civil War pistols, rifles, swords. Buy your merchandise from other gun dealers, at auctions, from families selling the old homestead or plantation. *Minimum starting capital: $3,000.*

3. UNUSUAL RECORDINGS for education or entertainment pay big returns. Educational courses on a variety of subjects lend themselves to either platter or tape recordings. You can often combine the recording with a book, giving the student two chances to learn. Typical subjects

include salesmanship, stock-market techniques, refrigeration, and similar topics. In the entertainment field you can produce your own music, vocal renditions, humor, or off-beat caricatures. Many singing stars—Bobby Vinton, Neal Sedaka, Anita Bryant, Frankie Avalon, Bobby Vee—run profitable sidelines. Some of these include recordings of their own songs. *Minimum starting capital: $10,000.*

4. TREE GROWING in your spare time can bring excellent profits if you enjoy working with products from the soil. Trees will conserve the soil *and* bring you an income. Evergreens, popular for Christmas trees, are easy to grow and do not require too much attention. Today nearly five million Americans cultivate small and large woodlots. Some part-time woodlot farmers believe they derive larger profits from their trees than from investing in stocks and bonds. Trees, however, require more attention than blue-chip stocks and bonds. Your state, the U.S. Forest Service, and American Forest Products Industries, Inc., can supply useful guidance on how and where to invest in a woodlot. *Minimum starting capital: $1,000.*

5. PART-TIME FARMING is on the rise because it offers a second income, a residence outside town, and healthful relaxation. One part-time farmer is a carpenter during his regular business hours. His wife raises white mice in the barn he renovated; her net income from sale of the mice is about $8,000 per year. For best results from part-time farming, choose a property that is in good condition. Pay a little more for the farm, if necessary. You'll be happy you did because good equipment helps the hens produce better eggs and the cows better milk. *Minimum starting capital: $5,000.*

6. PRIVATE INVESTIGATION, for a fee, can be a rewarding part-time activity. Many correspondence courses are available if you have no previous investigating experience. To gain as much experience as possible, you'll find it wise to accept all assignments offered during your first year in business. Once you know which types of work you like best you can begin to specialize. *Minimum starting capital (including education and office space): $1,500.*

7. PERSONAL COUNSELING is a useful and profitable source of a second income. You can advise people in any area of life about which you have specialized knowledge. Typical useful areas include college entrance, family relations, matrimonial problems, foreign-language accomplishments,

recreation, and similar topics. E. G. Osborne, well-known author and teacher, was also active in family counseling throughout the world. Note that in some states you must have a license to do certain types of counseling. Such licenses are not difficult to obtain if you have the required education and experience. *Minimum starting capital: $2000.*

8. TRAVEL AGENCY operation is well suited to part-time hours. Most travel agencies do little business before noon; many are active during the evening hours. You can buy an agency for $10,000 or more, or you can found your own agency. Since most people like to come to the agency to plan their trips, you'll need an attractive store. If you live in the suburbs, consider a scheme I heard of on the West Coast. A travel agent there fitted the interior of a van-type auto as a travel agency. In the evenings he visits nearby neighborhoods, inviting people to view the interior of the van. Many people are so intrigued with the posters, travel folders, and financing plans that they sign for a trip before leaving the van. This agent often serves coffee and cake in the van to keep people from leaving when they get hungry. "A bite to eat puts them into a better signing mood," the owner says. *Minimum starting capital: $10,000.*

9. HOME CONSTRUCTION is booming and will continue to expand as more new families seek a home of their own. A good friend of mine, who is a draftsman during the day, operates a part-time construction company. He hires carpenters, plumbers, and electricians in *their* spare time. In this way he finishes, and sells, about six houses per year. When his part-time help is laid off from other jobs they work full-time for him. He saves money on wages because the part-time craftsmen are glad to work for less than half the union rate. *Minimum starting capital: $10,000; be sure to obtain some experience or education before investing.*

10. RUG AND UPHOLSTERY CLEANING is a simple but lucrative business. Several firms sell excellent equipment, making your task easier. With the scarcity of servants today you can easily find more clients than you can service. Ads in your local paper will often bring many responses. Working out of your home, you can start with as little as $500; but to build a sizeable income you must invest more. *Minimum starting capital: $1,000.*

11. EXPORT-IMPORT BUSINESS is challenging and profitable. Dealers who buy your exports overseas are often willing to give you a good discount on the products of their country which you can import. Thus, the

two functions—export and import—can often be combined. Or, if you prefer, you can deal solely in either import or export. Either way, concentrate on products you know, from countries you know. That way there's less chance of being led astray by offers of faulty products which may fail to perform well in the U.S. or foreign markets. *Minimum starting capital: $8,000.*

12. OVERSEAS RENTALS have real dollar power. You serve as the U.S. representative of European, South American, Asian, and other homeowners who want to rent their homes to Americans for part of the year. Information you supply the prospective renter includes number of rooms, their size, type of heating system, number of baths, number of servants, rental charge, location with respect to the center of town, types of neighbors, and similar data. You collect the rent in advance, deduct your fee, and send the balance to the overseas owner. This is an ideal service-type business because the investment required is moderate and you can do all the work in your spare time. *Minimum starting capital: $2,000.*

13. FINDING ROOMMATES for people who move to large cities is an ideal way to build your spare-time second-income fortune. In operating a roommate business you charge a basic registration fee (say $5) for each person requesting your services. When you find a suitable roommate—after matching items like interests, religious preference, dating habits, type of work, and similar factors—an additional charge of $25, or more, is made *each* roommate. Thus, if you find 100 roommates your gross income is $3,000. Once you are established in a big city you should be able to find 250 to 500 roommates per year in your spare time. Your income from this activity will then range between $7,500 and $15,000. *Minimum starting capital: $3,000.*

14. PROVIDE TRANSPORTATION to interesting places. You can use almost any means to provide the transportation—car, bus, boat, airplane, horse, even mule. Reverend Eilif Krogager, a minister, wanted to offer his parishioners low-cost transportation to foreign countries. His first trip was so successful that he formed Sterling Airways. Within two years the company was operating four DC-6B's, and flew nearly 150 million passenger miles in its first year. When choosing a method of transportation, look for the popular, economical, and quick means first. You may find that this is the preferred method; or perhaps people may be tired of jet speeds and ready for a slow-boat-to-China ride. *Minimum starting capital: $25,000.*

15. OPEN A SCHOOL in the U.S., or elsewhere. If you're a teacher and are free during the summer, an overseas school for teenagers might be just right for you. As a job-holder you may want to teach your career specialty—plumbing, navigation, Spanish, kennel operation, or any of hundreds of others—to people in your area. Advertise in local papers and in magazines devoted to your field. The enrollment may be larger than you expect. *Minimum starting capital: $3,000.*

16. RUN A DELIVERY SERVICE for specialized products: theatre tickets, candy, shop-at-home stores, flowers. When starting you'll probably run most of the errands yourself. But once you know which products you want to specialize in, you can hire high school and college students to work in their spare time. With this type of help your labor costs will be lower. *Minimum starting capital: $3,000.*

17. BE A MANUFACTURER'S REPRESENTATIVE in your local area. Pick products you are interested in and know something about. Set up a definite schedule for answering the questions that arise about your products. Have this schedule printed and distribute it to your clients and prospects. Then you'll be able to service your clients at times that are convenient to you. *Minimum starting capital: $5,000.*

18. SELL USEFUL PRODUCTS like footwear, air conditioners, vending machines, greeting cards, auto parts, and other specialty products in your spare time. There are many products available today that are ideal for spare-time selling. Choose only quality items; don't waste your time and energy on cheap items people will throw away in disgust. High-quality products are easier to sell and pay you a higher commission. Also, your customers will be happier and repeat sales will be easier. *Minimum starting capital: $3,000.*

19. ANTIQUE UTENSILS command high prices, can be easily purchased at country auctions and similar sales. Thus, 19th century coffee grinders may sell for as much as $25 each. Paul Revere type lamps sell for $35; kitchen scales $17.50. An antique utensil shop in New York is run by a travel writer and a photographer as a spare-time business. One year after opening the store had to be moved to larger quarters because the demand for the utensils was so great. *Minimum starting capital: $3,000.*

20. PUBLISH A SPECIALIZED MAGAZINE if you have a business or professional interest that is not now served by a suitable publication. You can start small, in newsletter form. A friend of mine did just that, beginning with a newsletter for which he charged $84 per year. He hopes his circulation will grow to a level where he can expand to a broader treatment of his subject. Meanwhile, he earns a good income from the newsletter. *Minimum starting capital: $8,000.*

SPECULATION IN MODERATE-CAPITAL VENTURES PAYS OFF

Many people think speculation is a nasty word. It isn't; our country was built on the desire and with the power of speculation. Today we are the wealthiest and strongest nation in the world. When you speculate you work with dollar power, the greatest force available to build a spare-time second-income fortune.

In our great country you can speculate in thousands of ways. One of the simplest, from the standpoint of capital investment, is the stock market. You have no rent—a broker will gladly allow you to share his board room. No employees are necessary; neither are light, heat, or office supplies. You're the boss; you can take a vacation in January or June, or both—the stock market will still be there when you return. Best of all, your starting capital need not be large; but you do need the speculative fever—the desire to use your knowledge and mind to earn a large profit.

Making money as a stock-market speculator isn't easy. You must have the ability to analyze the market accurately, without allowing your emotions to rule your decisions. Some people, sensing the difficulty of making a profit in the market without analytical ability, turn to one or more of the activities described in this chapter.

Careful speculation in a moderate-capital venture of the type described in this chapter can pay off. Your profits can be high, *and* you may develop the analytical ability that will make you a top-notch stock-market speculator. Try it and see.

Many well-known sports figures, whose professional earning career may be short, turn to a spare-time second income during their playing years. These sports greats look forward to the time when they will no longer be able to play actively. When that time comes they hope that what was once a spare-time income will become a full-time business. These men and women speculate, risking today's money on future growth of their spare-time business. If they are willing to invest time, energy, and money in moderate-capital ventures, this shows their faith in the future. You, too, can build your fortune with a spare-time business that expands from a moderate beginning to a major success.

What's your hobby? Golf, hunting, boating, swimming, tennis, horseback riding, skin diving, surfing, flying, archery, antique cars, shell collecting, ham radio, photography, travel, or any of hundreds of others? Almost any hobby can, with a little ingenuity, be turned into a profitable spare-time second income.

Combine peace of mind with wealth building. You'll enjoy your work more and you'll be less tense at the end of the day. Here are six advantages of combining hobbies with spare-time fortune building.

12

Combine Hobbies

with Your

Second-Income Fortune

1. *Rid yourself of the leisure guilt.* Many Americans, raised on the Horatio Alger concept of success, can't relax. Good friends of mine, many of them highly successful businessmen, feel guilty when they're away from their work for more than a few hours. They carry a fat briefcase home every night, ignoring their families from the time dinner is finished until they go to bed. Why? Because they have a leisure guilt; they're unhappy unless working.

A hobby is a subject or pursuit you follow for fun. When you first take up a hobby you seldom consider earning money from it. As you become better acquainted with the hobby, many spare-time money-making opportunities may occur to you. If you can combine your hobby and second-income fortune search you will rid yourself of leisure guilt while building a profitable source of funds. Later in this chapter you'll discover many ways to convert a hobby into a good spare-time income.

2. *Be with people you enjoy.* Hobbyists enjoy being with other people having the same interests. If you don't believe this, spend some time in a golf course locker room, a boatyard, or at a stamp collector's convention. You'll see many happy faces—and you'll probably hear a few tall tales. When you combine a hobby with your search for a spare-time second-income fortune you associate with people who speak your special language, people who think the way you do. You derive joy from being with them and your work is more fun. And in many cases you'll find your work is more profitable.

3. *Do what brings you pleasure.* Many people toil for years, hating their work. If you dislike your work you have fewer chances of major success. Why labor for years at an unpleasant job when you can do what brings you pleasure? Some second-income fortune builders do menial work during the day. At night they work at a stimulating hobby, earning a profitable second income while deriving a deep satisfaction from their work. As one spare-time fortune builder told me, "The pleasure I get from working at my hobby in the evening gives me strength to face the drudgery of the next day." Many men build enough wealth during the evening to enable them to quit the drudgery of their daily jobs.

4. *Do what you do well.* Many hobbyists are more adept at their

hobby than they are at their jobs. Why? Because a hobby is fun, is interesting, and is absorbing. Hobbyists have a natural flair for their pursuit. Combine your spare-time second-income fortune with a favorite hobby and you'll earn more while having more fun. Do what you do well and the money will roll in faster than you ever thought possible.

5. *Enjoy your hobby at a lower cost.* With an income from your hobby you can enjoy it at little or no cost. Thus, a friend of mine loves horseback riding. For years he paid high fees for the care and feeding of his favorite nag. Then he heard of a small riding stable offered for sale. Borrowing some money, he bought the stable. Today the stable returns a profitable second income, and instead of having one horse, my friend has ten. He rides whenever he wants to—at no expense. Instead of one animal "eating him out of house and home," he's eating off the profits of ten horses.

There are many other ways you can enjoy your hobby at a lower cost. The expert golfer can give lessons; the boatowner can, after obtaining the necessary license, take out fishing parties; the stamp collector can sell or trade his prized items. Earn a little or a lot from your hobby and you can enjoy the best of hobbies at the lowest prices.

6. *Build for retirement fun while you acquire a fortune.* Your retirement can be a nightmare of low income, few interests and no friends. Turn your hobby into an income and you overcome the nightmarish aspects of retirement by earning more money, acquiring broader interests and many friends. A writer friend of mine retired to live on his boat. Once he got the boat into tip-top shape he was lost—he didn't know what to do in the morning. In the afternoon he swam; in the evening he lounged on his deck, drinking beer and playing cards. He decided to "come out of retirement" in the morning and write boating articles for magazines. Today he is a happy man. visiting other boats for ideas, writing them up, and deriving a second income from them.

You, too, can build for retirement. The spare-time second-income you build today will make your retirement more secure. The interests and friends you develop will keep you active, alert, and healthy. Can anyone ask for more? You can't beat current income which helps with today's budget and builds future securitv.

YOU CAN FIND OPPORTUNITIES IN YOUR HOBBY

Obtain financial data about your hobby. Thus, 40 million people took part in boating activities in the United States in a recent year. They spent $2.5 billion on their hobby. A magazine serving the model-railroading hobby estimates that 300 new hobbyists enter the field every week, spending nearly $100 each to get started. About 4.5 million people ski in the United States every winter. If each person spends $100 per winter on ski equipment, lessons, or other fees, the total outlay is $450 million. This is enough to make any businessman interested.

Collect financial data on your hobby from magazines serving the hobbyist, *The Wall Street Journal, Business Week,* and similar publications. By contacting the advertising department of the biggest hobby magazine in your field you can obtain much useful information—number of people in the hobby, average annual expenditure, items on which the money is spent, and similar useful information.

Analyze the financial data you obtain and see if there is a need you can fill at a profit to yourself. Study the growth trend in your hobby. Some hobbies, like golf, grow every year. Others, like boating and bowling, grow for awhile and then level off for a few years. Then they begin to grow again. Translate growth trends into dollar trends and profit potentials for yourself.

Estimate your chances for success. Study the hobby thoroughly to learn if your service or product is needed, practical, unique, and reasonable enough to be bought in sufficient quantities to pay you a modest profit. If your product or service meets these four requirements, get to work, using the hints given in this and the other chapters in this book. Profit from your hobby in your spare time—there is no better way of enjoying the pleasures of a hobby and the benefits of a second-income fortune. Now let's look at many of the hobbies you can turn into a profitable sideline activity.

GOLF BOOMS BY DAY AND BY NIGHT

All of America is golf crazy, and England, Japan, France, Germany, and many other countries aren't far behind us in this love of the little white ball. Throughout the United States golf courses are jammed on weekdays and weekends. Some 18-hole courses are so overloaded with players that they are installing floodlights on greens and fairways to permit round-the-clock golf. Golf pros estimate that some courses will soon stay open 24 hours a day—and even then some players will have to wait before they can tee off. There are now nearly 7 million golfers in the United States, or about 820 players on each 18-hole course.

Overcrowding of 18-hole courses drives people to smaller courses like the par-three (pitch-and-putt), miniature, and indoor courses. Driving ranges allow people to practice their long shots at little expense. The latest invention—indoor electronic golf machines—allows you to "play" any well-known course in the world, using your own clubs, a real ball, and full swings. You do all of this indoors, air-conditioned in the summer, heated in winter—without walking.

Your best investments in golf today are in the smaller course, driving ranges, golf machines and golf equipment. You can run a spare-time second-income business in any of these and earn profits of $15,000 or more per year. Operating a full-size 18-hole course is almost impossible for the spare-time fortune builder unless you buy land 50 miles from town. Then you won't have enough customers to pay the cost of greens sprinkling. Also, your total investment can run to nearly $500,000. This is too much for the typical spare-time fortune builder.

Watch the business columns of your newspaper for ads for small courses. You can often take over a par-three or miniature course with a down payment of only $2,000. Driving ranges run a little higher, usually $5,000. Indoor miniature courses can be bought for $2,000 to $4,000 down, depending on location. You can often borrow the down payment if you follow the hints in Chapter 5.

Golf machines are currently controlled by franchise. Watch the columns of *The Wall Street Journal* for offers of a franchise in your area. Some franchise firms offer financing help, advice on location, and many other useful services.

Golf equipment can be a lucrative spare-time business for you. Arnold Palmer, the well-known and highly talented professional golfer, is said to operate some forty enterprises bringing him an annual income of some $500,000. His products include a camera to check your swing, golf clubs, bags, balls and clothes. You may be able to develop a useful golf product that will have a wide market. If your hobby is golf you are almost certain to have developed a handy item other golfers might like to use. Follow the hints in Chapters 8 and 9 to convert your product into a profitable spare-time second income.

One aspect of the golf business that puzzles new spare-time fortune builders is where to find help. This is one of the easiest problems to solve. There are thousands of teenagers who will be delighted to work on your small golf course for modest wages. These kids are willing, honest, and talented. They form an easily tapped labor pool that will solve most of your problems. Check your local high school for boys interested in working on a golf course.

BOATING IS AMERICA'S BIGGEST SUMMER SPORT

Forty million people owning seven million boats can't be wrong. Boating is a *big* sport, popular from coast to coast and on inland lakes and rivers. What opportunities are open to you as a boating hobbyist? There are many. You can rent boats, operate a marina, charter your boat, sell or manufacture boating accessories, or run charter cruises. These activities can be pursued in northern climates during the summer and southern climates during the northern winter. Or, if you wish, you can confine your activities to one area and work in your spare time for only half the year.

For best results in the boating field, start small and expand with the increased demand for your services. I did this in the boating accessories field, starting with one calculator which I gave the tradename "Pilot-Aid." Demand for the calculator was so large and so steady that nine more Pilot-Aids were developed. Today there is a complete line of ten calculators serving the boatman's needs. These products are sold by mail order, by the marine-supply stores, by boatyards, and similar outlets.

In any boating business, avoid a large investment in machinery, equipment, land, or supplies when first starting. The demand for boating services and products can, and does, fluctuate sharply. If you invest a large part of your capital in expensive equipment or land you may find you are short of cash. Your safest bet when starting your business is to rent or lease needed equipment or land. When manufacturing a product use job-shop factories or freelance help. This way you pay only for what you receive. The costs of machine depreciation, maintenance, and operation are paid by the factory, not by you.

It is possible to combine several marine activities and earn a profit while enjoying your hobby. Thus, one boating enthusiast purchased a new fiberglass sailboat from the manufacturer at a 30 per cent discount (the usual discount given boat dealers begins at 20 per cent). He also agreed to demonstrate the boat in his local area and take orders. The hobbyist and his family were thus able to enjoy a summer on the water at a lower cost while having an opportunity to earn a profit.

During the first summer he had the boat this spare-time second-income fortune builder sold seven sailboats for a total profit of $3,500. The second summer he took prospective buyers on three-day cruises, upping his sales to ten boats for a total of seventeen in two years. You may question his initial investment in the boat. Doesn't this violate the earlier recommendation of not using a large part of your capital for equipment? No, because this hobbyist wanted a boat for relaxation and would have bought one whether or not there was a profit potential. Becoming a floating dealer allowed him to purchase the boat at a good discount and also earn a profit from it.

Some real enthusiasts cruise all over the world, carrying paying passengers. The income from the passengers is more than enough to pay all expenses with enough left over for a modest profit. The schooner *Yankee* operated this way for many years, making round-the-world trips carrying young men and women who helped steer, navigate, and maintain the vessel. However, most part-time businessmen prefer to stay closer to home.

If you like boats there's money to be made around, on, and with them. Just keep your eyes open while you're in a boatyard, marine store, and marina. Ideas are everywhere; you can earn money while enjoying yourself if you put a good idea to work.

YOU CAN BEAT THE HORSES

Some men spend all their lives trying to beat the horses by placing bets at the $2 window. Few ever win; fewer break even; most lose more than they can afford. If you have a perfect "system" for beating the horses, skip this section. But if you're still searching for a good system, read on—you may find it here.

Riding stables earn excellent profits for their owners. The stable also gives you plenty of opportunity to ride, if riding is your hobby. You can start a riding stable on a farm, vacant lot, or any other piece of ground. A barn can be easily converted to a stable, or you can erect a small pre-fabricated building to house the horses. People are willing to drive to a stable, so your land cost will be low if you pick a spot on the outskirts of town. Try to choose land in an area having several schools because teen-age girls are prime customers for many riding stables.

Begin with two or three horses. If you're unsure of your profit po-tential, rent the land instead of buying it. Advertise the stable in local papers; distribute handbills in local junior and senior high schools. A well-run riding stable will return you a profit of $1 to $2 per hour rental time per horse. With three horses and 2,000 hours per year rental time your profit will range from $6,000 to $12,000. This is one sure way of beating the horses.

Many riding-stable owners, as well as almost every man who ever bet $2 on a horse, dream of owning a "fast nag." For what better way to beat the horses than to own a stake-winning horse? You can even bet on him, if you know his chances are good.

Owning a race horse isn't a low-cost business. But it can be highly profitable—or extremely disappointing. Fred Turner, the oil scout who struck it rich by claiming survey vacancies, paid $6,762 for Tomy Lee, a horse he planned to use as a traveling companion for another race horse he owned named Tuleg. Tomy Lee became a top winner, earning $377,117 in two years. He won the 1959 Kentucky Derby.

Some race horses sell for as low as $300; others go for $3,500. Promis-ing yearlings go for as high as $25,000.

If you're seriously interested in owning a race horse, begin by buying a "piece" of one—that is, becoming a part owner. You can learn a great deal about racing profits, and losses, this way without investing too much capital.

Trotters, becoming more popular every year, do not require as large an investment as race horses. Your winnings will usually be less, though they can be steadier because the trotting season is longer. To get information about trotters, spend some time around the stables at a local track. Trotter owners are frequently selling and trading horses. You can usually find an owner who will sell you a piece of one of his horses for a modest investment of $500 to $5,000. If trotting is your hobby you'll enjoy owning a few horses, and with wise choices you can earn a good spare-time second income from your horses.

Hunt clubs combine horses, dogs, and rifles. These clubs are popular in many areas. To organize a club you need land, and plenty of it. Many spare-time hunt-club operators start on rented land because this eliminates the need for a large capital investment. Other operators buy large tracts of land with little money down—say $2,000 to $5,000—and regard the monthly mortgage payment as the equivalent of rent. Often you can organize a club, collect initiation fees in advance and use this money as a down payment or rental fee. With an interesting and challenging terrain you need not invest in horses or dogs, since people will bring their own. While hunt clubs can be profitable the income is usually earned only during the hunting season, unless you supply your own animals for the chase. Even then, your state government may require that you obtain a special permit.

TWELVE OTHER PROFITABLE HOBBY VENTURES

SKIN AND SCUBA DIVING offers many chances for fun and profit. Two friends of mine, Roy and June Keiser, mix fun and a second income by teaching skin and scuba diving at a nearby diving school. Roy usually teaches the water skills while June gives classroom instruction. Other scuba divers enjoy their hobby while diving for treasure. One company, formed to salvage sunken World War II cargo vessels, wined and dined German submarine captains to gather details about ships they torpedoed. Talented scuba divers often write books and articles about their hobby. Still others open skin and scuba supply stores selling diving products to hobbyists. A few even manufacture specialty products for divers. These products are sold through dive shops and mail order. Another group of divers specializes in salvaging items like outboard motors, autos, and other valuables. Regardless of your interests, skin and scuba diving offer you health and income potential if you practice the rules of safe diving and swimming. *Minimum starting capital: $100 to $5,000.*

SURFING, the craze of the west coast, has moved east. Today you'll find surfboards wherever there are waves large enough to propel a man shorewards. In surfing you can sell boards, rent them, make repairs, give lessons, and enter contests. Your best opportunities as an amateur surfer are in sales and service. Here your knowledge of general surfing techniques will be useful when you sell equipment to new surfers. To give surfing lessons you should have more skill and want an activity that keeps you physically active. Repairing surfboards does not bring a steady income and is best combined with equipment sales. *Minimum starting capital: $500 to $3,000.*

ANTIQUE CARS provide part-time profits for hot-rodders, young and old. Car restoration is exciting, challenging, and profitable. You may have to chase over three states to find a 1909 bumper for one of your classic cars. If auto restoration doesn't interest you then try acting as agent for people interested in buying or selling antique cars. You can also write articles or books about famous cars of the past and present. Floyd Clymer, the famous auto expert, authors popular books on antique cars that are avidly received by hobbyists throughout the world. If you have a large barn or garage which can house six or more cars, consider converting it to an antique-car museum. The admission fees can pay your expenses and give you a modest profit. *Minimum starting capital: $500 to $5,000.*

ARCHERY RANGES are shooting for high profits today, indoors and outdoors. Outdoor ranges require little investment—$500 can get you started on a rented strip of land. Indoor ranges are more elaborate and require a larger investment, usually $10,000 or more. Automatic ranges are presently offered as franchises with the possibility of financing assistance. *Minimum starting capital: $500 to $10,000.*

PRIVATE FLYING is a growth hobby because the auto industry is turning out more cars than ever before, causing people to take to the skies to "get away from it all." You can fly passengers for hire, give flying lessons, form a flying club, or perform special tasks like taking aerial photos, flying freight for small companies, or working at local parachute-jumping and similar exhibitions. All you need for most of these services is a reliable plane. Many used but serviceable planes are available for as little as $800. If you recondition such a plane yourself you can then form a club and recover all, or part, of your investment via initiation fees. You can use this money to buy another plane which can be put to work for any of the services suggested above. Of course, you must have the necessary licenses, but if you are interested in flying they are easy to obtain. To find customers for the various services you offer, place ads in local papers. *Minimum starting capital: $1,000 to $3,000.*

HI-FI is an excellent indoor hobby having high profit potentials. You can service hi-fi sets, install them, advise prospective customers, and sell equipment in your local area. Your success depends upon a good knowledge of the principles and equipment of this growing hobby. The man who earns the greatest spare-time income in this hobby is the one who knows more than his customers. So acquire as much knowledge as possible before opening your business. *Minimum starting capital: $500 to $5,000.*

PRO RADIO can be lucrative if you combine knowledge of radio with another service. Thus, a friend of mine earns a steady fee from several wealthy boat owners. All this pro does is broadcast the complete stock-market tables to the boat owners five days a week while these men are cruising. If they want a special quotation on a stock they simply call him and he contacts a broker. He also places buy and sell orders, as requested. There are many other ways in which you can use pro radio equipment to earn money. You can assist local taxi and industrial firms, communicate with hunters, sportsmen, and other groups that are beyond the reach of a telephone. *Minimum starting capital: $500 to $3,000.*

PHOTOGRAPHY is always booming, particularly as more men and women graduate from college, marry, have children, and reach other milestones in their lives. Take your pick of a photo specialty—children, weddings, graduations, parties, industrial shots, or any of many others. You'll find that people are always looking for a new photographer who has a fresh viewpoint. Equipment costs can be as low as $250 when you start but they can run to $5,000, or more, if you need a large photo laboratory. Advertising costs are low; you can begin in low-cost local papers and magazines and expand from there as business grows. Also, you can set your working hours so your spare-time activities do not interfere with your regular job. *Minimum starting capital: $250 to $5,000.*

COIN COLLECTING is an expanding hobby which is finding new enthusiasts every day. People enjoy investing in valuable coins because the worth of the coin or bill continues to increase as time passes. Some experts state that you can earn from 50% to 200% per year by buying and holding new coins. You can't go wrong in coin collecting because the items you acquire have a certain worth in themselves. Thus, the 1900 silver dollar will always be worth at least one dollar. Some, like the "Morgan dollars," minted at the now-closed San Francisco, Carson City, or New Orleans mints, are valued at $30 to $1,500 each, depending on the year and rarity. Coin collecting does not require a large investment; all you need is about $200 and a determination to learn which coins are rare. Then you must hunt for them. *Minimum starting capital: $200 to $2,000.*

STAMP COLLECTING, like coin collecting, is a low-cost hobby requiring only a modest investment. Study the valuable stamps and then begin searching for them. A keen eye searching through a fifty-cent packet of stamps may discover a stamp worth $1, $2, $5, or more. Building a collection of "period" stamps, or a similar specialty, can give you a big payoff when you're ready to sell the album. Or you can, if you wish, sell stamps in bulk to other collectors. If writing about stamps interests you, publish a newsletter for collectors. The subscription price will be enough to permit you to show a profit. *Minimum starting capital: $50 to $2,000.*

MODEL BUILDING and operation is fun and profitable. Radio-controlled models are the most popular today. One of the leading builders of radio-controlled model boats in the United States today is Duke Nichols of Eagle Path, Texas. His models, ranging up to a 10-foot replica of the liner *France,* turn, stop, maneuver, and perform other operations at the flick of a switch. To earn money from models you can build, sell, service, or demonstrate them. Other models you might build include airplanes, cars, tanks, trains, guns, and houses. My wife, a talented builder of model houses, derives a profitable spare-time income designing and building model houses for home builders and architects. This hobby keeps her interested while she isn't writing a history book, which is another of her many spare-time activities. *Minimum starting capital: $100 to $1,000.*

PET RAISING is profitable fun if you like dogs, cats, rabbits, mice, or any of a number of other pets. Some pet raisers conduct their business in an apartment, raising only one or two pets at a time. Others have private homes or a farm and raise ten or a hundred, or more, pets at once. To start raising pets, choose your favorite animal and buy two or more from a reputable pet dealer. Obtain breeding certificates, if this is the practice. Study several books on correct breeding practices and follow their recommendations. If you raise strong, healthy pets you will soon have a good reputation and people will come to you again and again. *Minimum starting capital: $100 to $500.*

TURN YOUR HOBBIES INTO PROFITS

There are thousands of hobbies from which you can earn money.

Give each some thought and you can soon have a profitable sideline income. Use your hobbies to build your spare-time second-income fortune and you'll profit in two ways—your income will be larger and you'll get more fun out of life.

Most second-income fortune builders are cash-poor; they seldom have enough capital to build a thriving business. Some must work for years to overcome this cash shortage. Of course, many *do* overcome their cash shortage and go on to build a large fortune. But why should you slave to build capital if you can get it from the public? Today there are thousands of people in the United States anxious to invest money in profitable spare-time second-income ventures.

Many beginning fortune builders are

Bring the Public

in on Your

Second-Income Hunt

reluctant to give up a part-interest in their business, even for cash. "The public is trying to rob me," these fortune builders will say to you whenever someone offers to put some money into a project. Actually the public isn't trying to rob the fortune builder; the public just wants a piece of his good luck and is willing to pay for it.

There are four advantages to going public: (1) You have more capital than if you financed the business yourself. As head of the business you can make most of the decisions as to where and how this capital will be used. (2) There will be more talent for you to draw on because people who invest in your business will be happy to give advice. This advice will often be helpful. In fact, just having an interested person to talk to can be very helpful when you are first starting a business. (3) With a larger capital investment your profit potential is higher. This means you can reach your fortune goal sooner. Once you achieve your goal you can sit back and relax, or go on to build a larger fortune. (4) Your backers, since they've invested their money, will support your efforts with enthusiasm. Their interest and encouragement will spur you to greater efforts. Your chances for outstanding success will improve.

There are, of course, some disadvantages to selling the public a share of your business. But the disadvantages are minor compared with the advantages. Major disadvantages are: (1) You may have a number of people trying to tell you how to run your business. (2) It may be necessary for you to divulge facts and data about your business which you'd prefer to keep confidential. (3) There will be greater pressure on you to succeed because the money you are risking belongs to others. (4) Should you achieve outstanding success, you will have to share your wealth with the people who helped finance you.

Analyze these disadvantages and you'll find that none are serious. There are ways to keep control of a company or business while using capital supplied by outsiders. Many of these techniques are given later in this chapter.

HOW YOU CAN GO PUBLIC

There are three ways to bring outsiders into your business by means of a stock offering. Each has special features you'll want to consider.

1. A private offering of your stock, idea, or skill is an arrangement in which you sell a portion of the ownership (stock), part of the rights

to an idea, or the output of a certain skill to an individual or firm. The usual private offering is concluded without the general public being aware of the arrangement. You obtain the money (usually tax free) and can use it to expand your business.

Private purchase of stock in your company is usually made by a brokerage house. Most houses require that your business be operating and showing a profit before they will consider a private offering. Your business must also, of course, have future growth potential. If it doesn't have this potential there is little sense of investing more money in it.

You can also sell part of the rights to an idea or skill. Thus, one author I know of sold half the rights to his next five books for $50,000 to a private investor *before* the books were written. The $50,000 permits the author to concentrate on his writing without worrying about money. Freedom from money worries will enable him to write better, more salable material. As each book is written its earnings will repay a portion of the $50,000 investment, plus a nominal dividend.

An idea can be merchandised in a similar way. The first earnings from it will either repay the investor or will be shared with the investor on a percentage basis.

2. A limited public offering to twenty-five or fewer persons is usually called a private placement and need not be registered with the Securities and Exchange Commission (SEC). If you have a good idea you can often interest enough friends and relatives to buy stock in sufficient quantities to finance all, or part, of your business. To be completely sure of the rules governing a private placement in your state, consult a lawyer.

Private offerings are popular with people having a common interest or hobby. Thus, boat owners in one area recently formed a corporation to build a marina. Twenty owners each contributed $5,000 to provide a total capital of $100,000. A manager was appointed to supervise construction of the marina. When the project was finished each owner had a slip for his boat and received a portion of the profits earned by the marina. You can arrange similar financing for your business by applying the numbers of wealth, as shown in Chapter 7. Almost any worthwhile second-income business can be financed this way, if you plan wisely. Money obtained from a private-placement sale of stock is not subject to income taxes on the corporate tax return.

3. Regulation A stock offerings are those in which the total stock issued sells for $300,000 or less. Such an offering is easier to make than a

larger one because you do not have to provide too much information to the SEC. You can use the money obtained from such an offering to pay off previously acquired debts, build a plant, manufacture products, meet a payroll, or for any other purpose connected with your business.

You can use a Regulation A stock offering to finance any legitimate business venture organized as a corporation. Unusual small stock offerings include those made by a firm owning some twenty-five race horses, an underseas treasure-hunting firm, a uranium mine, a swimming-pool builder, a publisher of magazines serving tropical-fish hobbyists, a cookie baker, and hundreds of others.

Demands for new stock issues of untried companies vary with activity in the major stock markets. During 1961 there was a scramble by the investing public to buy new issues in all kinds of companies—particularly those planning to, or doing, business in the engineering and scientific fields. Prices of some issues doubled within a few days after the offering was made. The subsequent stock-market decline of May, 1962, discouraged many investors, scaring them out of the new-issues market.

The American public, however, loves a gamble. New issues will return to favor. If you have a good idea and are ready with a prospectus, there is an excellent chance to obtain up to $300,000 capital from the public. Write the United States Securities and Exchange Commission, Washington 25, D. C., and request a copy of "Regulation A. General Exemption." This excellent booklet provides much information on the steps to take in making a Regulation A offering.

MAKE THE MOST OF PUBLIC FUNDS

Don't squander money you obtain from the public. Put the money to good use; if you waste it your stockholders will be irritated and may try to eject you from the company. Here are five powerful hints for getting the most from public funds:

1. *Keep acquisition costs low.* Sell your own stock instead of paying a broker to sell it. This way you'll save twenty to thirty cents on every dollar's worth of stock you sell. A good friend of mine decided to go into the book-publishing business. Figuring that $75,000 to $100,000 was needed to start, he prepared his own prospectus and had it printed. He distributed this to his friends, and friends of friends. Within a few

months more than $100,000 was invested in the business. Today he is guiding a booming publishing firm.

To prepare a prospectus, follow the hints in the SEC booklet listed above. You can also use as a guide a prospectus issued by a firm similar to your own. When I prepared the prospectus for one of my firms I studied a dozen prospectuses issued by other small companies. By preparing the prospectus yourself you can save additional money.

2. *Keep careful expense records.* If you've never had a large sum of money before, there is a temptation to spend carelessly when you first receive the money from your Regulation A offering. Some beginning spare-time fortune builders think that with $100,000 to $300,000 cash in the bank it will be impossible to spend it all. This isn't true; one of the easiest tasks in the world is to spend money. To prevent wasting the funds you obtain, set up careful expense records to keep track of every penny that comes in and every penny you spend.

3. *Separate your funds* so you don't mix public money with your personal cash. With this arrangement you can keep more accurate records. Also, it will be easier for you to pay your taxes because you'll know exactly how much you spent on business activities.

4. *Use accurate and acceptable accounting methods* in your business. Pay an accountant to advise you on the best procedures for your business. Follow his advice. With the relatively large sums obtainable from a public offering, you need professional accounting advice to keep up to date about the newest accounting methods. Remember: a good accountant will often save you several times his fee.

5. *Use your funds to build a good credit rating.* Establish checking, savings, and revolving-credit accounts at a big, important bank. Visit the bank and get to know the vice president. Tell him how you are building a fortune in your spare time. Pay off your loans in advance. Keep a sizeable deposit, say $10,000, in a savings account where it will earn interest. With a good credit rating you will find it easy to borrow any extra funds you may need.

HOW TO GO BACK TO THE PUBLIC FOR MORE MONEY

As your business develops you may need more cash. If your firm is showing a profit and paying dividends to the stockholders you should be able to issue more stock at low cost. The easiest way to sell more stock is to issue warrants to existing stockholders. Warrants entitle the stockholders to buy additional shares of stock at a price below the existing market price. If there is a large enough difference, most stockholders will be willing to buy more shares in a profitable company.

You can justify the need for additional funds by citing the plans you have for the company. Show how large a profit you expect from the new business the extra capital will generate. Translate this into larger dividends and increased worth for the stockholder.

By issuing warrants you obtain new funds at lowest cost. Many of the largest companies in the United States use this fast, low-cost method to obtain new money to finance expansion and other expenses.

If your company hasn't shown a profit, but you believe it will after acquiring new funds, use the same procedure. Explain why a profit hasn't been shown yet. Then go on to show how the new funds will convert a loss to a gain. If you present convincing arguments, and can show growth by a reduction in losses, you have an excellent chance to obtain the money you need.

Guard your new funds carefully. Try to avoid mistakes you may have made with funds obtained from your initial financing. Put the money to work earning a profit and you have a good chance of making your stockholder's equity in the company grow.

Public funds can build your spare-time second-income fortune. Use the hints given in this chapter and you can earn money using other people's money. What nicer way is there to build a spare-time second-income fortune for yourself and your family?

14

"The taxes—they'll ruin you," said a spare-time second-income fortune builder. What he said is partially true for those fortune builders who neglect to keep themselves informed about the various federal and state tax laws affecting their business. You *can* live with our present tax laws, if you expend the time and energy to learn how to limit your taxes to the legal minimum. This chapter gives you many useful hints on how to plan your tax liabilities so you derive maximum income from your spare-time efforts.

Keep the Fortune
You Build

You can't deduct business expenses unless you're in business to show a profit. So the first step you must take is to establish your business. Do this by registering your business name, address, and principal activity in your county courthouse or other required office. Next, have letterheads, envelopes, calling cards, and similar business stationery prepared. The cost of registration and stationery will seldom exceed $50. If you'll need a telephone, have one installed and listed under your business name. Buy a desk, typewriter, files, and other needed office equipment, if you have the cash to invest. If you're short of cash, use a card table, several orange crates, or any other suitable substitute.

Many a successful full-time business starts spare-time in a garage or basement and grows into a flourishing factory. The great electronics firm, Hewlett-Packard, began in an old garage. Herman Schaevitz, an engineer, began an electronics business in his basement; today his highly successful firm is in a modern building in Camden, New Jersey. Samuel Cohn, an immigrant to the United States, went to college at night. In his spare time he ran metallurgical experiments in his tenement apartment. Here he invented the gas mantle which brought him an income of several million dollars. Charles Simmons, Jr., founder and president of Simmons Machine Tool Corporation and Simmons Fastener Corporation, worked in the evenings at home to improve the tools he worked with as a machinist. With capital of $200 and the design of a new drill socket he developed, he went into business. His plant grew to occupy forty acres containing twelve large buildings.

You needn't form a corporation to begin a business, unless your lawyer advises you to do so. Certain types of businesses are better operated in the corporate form from their beginning. Since conditions vary so widely it is impossible to generalize. For best results, see your lawyer.

BUSINESS DEDUCTIONS YOU SHOULD CONSIDER

Obtain a good tax guide and study it. The United States Government Printing Office *Tax Guide for Small Business*, issued every year, is excellent. Study every page of this or any similar tax guide to learn the many business deductions the law allows you.

Typical deductions you may be allowed include: a portion of your home expenses when you have an office in your home (light, heat, repairs, depreciation), auto expenses for car or truck used in business, books and magazines needed for business, tools, uniforms, business travel and entertainment. There are hundreds of other legitimate deductions you can uncover by a careful study of the latest tax laws.

"Deductions are fine," you say, "but what happens if they are disallowed?" Legitimate deductions won't be disallowed *if you keep adequate records*. Thus, if you conduct business in your home, save every business letter addressed to your home. Keep a diary of visits of business people to your home. If you use your auto partly for business and partly for pleasure keep an exact record of the mileage driven for business purposes. Record where you drove, and why. Note which business deal was made.

T & E—travel and entertainment expenses—can be deducted, if you meet the requirements of the Internal Revenue Service. The keys to T & E expenses are receipts and records; try to obtain a receipt for every travel and entertainment expenditure you make. A receipt is required for every item of $25 or more. Keep a record of every entertainment item—list the date, place (restaurant, hotel), person, his title and firm name, business purpose, and business discussion. With adequate records you will be able to prove all T & E deductions you claim.

There are hundreds of other deductions to which you may be entitled because you run a spare-time second-income business. The best way to learn about these is by study of a tax guide. A few typical business deductions worth your study are: accident insurance premiums, accounting costs, advertising fees, alteration costs for business purposes, bad debts, bank fees, bookkeeping costs, casualty losses of business property, cost of cleaning offices and manufacturing facilities, cost of collecting income, cost of tax advice, damages to business property depreciation costs of business property, dues paid to business and professional organizations, exhibits for product sale or publicity, experimental costs, farming expenses when this is a spare-time business, fire-insurance premiums, gasoline taxes paid on fuel for business auto, heating costs for office, income taxes paid to a state, interest on business loans, labor costs, license fees, losses sustained in business, magazines serving your business activity, office rent and maintenance, postage for business letters and packages, real estate taxes, business office and plant supplies, telephone and telegraph costs, dues for unions related to your business. Knowing your legal deductions can save you money. This means you'll keep more of the spare-time second income you earn, so begin now to learn the details of the Federal and state tax laws affecting your business.

CONSIDER VARIOUS ORGANIZATION FORMS

Most beginning second-income fortune builders operate as sole proprietors, but a partnership or corporation may be a better form for your business. Much depends on the type of business. Thus, a friend of mine repairs watches and clocks in his spare time. Since there is little need for outside help he operates as a sole proprietor. Another friend owns several seagoing freighters. Because he has a large investment and the liability of loss is always present, he operates his business as a corporation.

Sometimes the corporate form of business can save taxes. Much depends on the amount of income from your regular job and the tax bracket you are in. Study your tax guide; if you need further advice see a tax lawyer or accountant—his fee, in general, is deductible.

When you have a large family you may be able to assign part of your income to your children and thereby reduce your tax burden. Thus, you can assign up to $599 to each child and the child will not have to pay any income tax on the income. The money, however, must remain in the possession of the child. You cannot transfer the money to a child and then take the money back and expect to avoid taxes. Your assignment of income must be a valid arrangement.

When you have a large spare-time income, which we hope you will, consider forming a trust to which you assign all or part of your income. The most common arrangement used by second-income fortune builders is the *short-term trust*. With this type of trust you transfer your property to a trustee for ten years or more. During this time the trust pays income taxes on the income received. At the end of ten years the property is returned to you. If it has appreciated in value you can sell it and pay taxes at the lower capital-gains rate. See your attorney for full details on setting up a trust.

Consider assigning some of your income to relatives other than your children, if they are in the lower tax brackets. Thus, you might assign income to your mother, father, aunts or uncles. With a smaller income than your own, they will pay a lower tax than you would and more of the money will be available for use by members of the family.

Invest some of your spare-time income in high-grade tax-exempt bonds. These bonds are sold to raise money for highways, municipal waterworks, and similar public facilities. Most bonds of this type yield a return of 3⅓ to 3½ per cent. When your income taxes are in the 35 per cent bracket a 3½ per cent tax-exempt yield gives you as much net income as a 5 per cent taxable yield.

Before your income taxes become a major problem, subscribe to a reliable tax service. Read the bulletins regularly. Start a tax notebook. Enter in this notebook data on tax laws affecting your business. Be tax conscious every day of the year. Make full use of the legal deductions to which you are entitled. Above all, report every cent of spare-time income. Don't cheat—you'll regret it. For if you report *all* your income, and claim only those deductions to which you are entitled, there is little chance of being slapped with an unforeseen tax deficiency.

INVEST YOUR SPARE-TIME INCOME

Don't allow your fortune to depreciate—invest it. Pyramid your second income to make a small fortune earn a big fortune. Take the money you earn from a steady job and invest it in a risky but high-return spare-time business. Use the profit from this business to invest in blue-chip stocks, government bonds, and other safe securities; or invest in luxury apartment houses and similar safe real estate properties.

Can you pyramid from risky to less risky investments? Certainly you can; it's being done every day. Thus, a lawyer turns his hobby of mathematics into a profitable spare-time income by inventing a planning board that substitutes for a computer. He builds the first board in his basement at home. Today he is president of a successful company selling his products to several industries. Income from this business is invested in profitable blue-chip company securities, and other worthwhile ventures. An advertising executive teams with his wife to found a club catering to people interested in visiting tropical islands. The husband-and-wife team loves visiting out-of-the-way islands and reporting their findings to members of their club. They save their profits, investing them for the future.

There are thousands of others. The railroad conductor who imports Hong Kong junks for sale in the United States; the university professor who opened a jazz hall and now lives off its profits; the author who prepared a correspondence course for supermarket employees and has an active school going full blast; the chef who bought a night club, featuring two restaurants, a bar, and dance floor, in a popular ski resort; the marine surplus dealer who buys aging ships, finds a cargo for the last voyage, and has the ship towed—full of cargo—to the scrap yard. Profit from the cargo pays the towing expenses; the scrapping income pays the profits. All these businessmen are building profits for the future, developing an income today that will take care of their needs several years from now.

For my own spare-time income, which comes from a variety of sources, I find blue-chip stock and bond investments best. By confining my purchases to the best companies much risk is eliminated. At the start of each year I estimate how the stocks and bonds I hold will perform. I do this by estimating how much the price will rise and what the dividend return will be. Each morning I check the performance in the stock-market tables of the newspaper. Though I mentally establish a stop-loss level at which I will sell the stock, I have never yet had to sell a stock to prevent a loss of capital.

In choosing stocks I look for blue-ribbon growth opportunities. Thus, I'd buy a New York Stock Exchange listed company in preference to any unlisted, unknown company. "This limits profits," you say. True, but it also gives me more protection for those important spare-time second-income dollars. Safe pyramiding of spare-time dollars brings peace of mind and a sense of well-being.

KEEP PUSHING TO BUILD YOUR FORTUNE

Expand and diversify your investments as your income increases. Don't invest in wild schemes; keep your head, and your second-income fortune. When you have money people will hound you with projects in which they think you should invest. Analyze those projects that interest you. Don't waste time on the others. Keep one fact in mind at all times: *It's much easier to spend money than to earn it.* Keep what you have; invest it only when you're sure you have a good venture.

Trust your own judgment. If you're smart enough to build a spare-time second-income fortune you have enough brains to determine how to pyramid your money.

Protect your fortune in life—and death. If you don't have a will, see a lawyer immediately. Explain your situation to him. Have him prepare a will that protects your family and your business. Where your fortune is large, and I hope that it is, obtain advice on estate taxes. With planning you can pass a major portion of your estate on to your survivors. Death is unpleasant, but we all must plan for it.

Be sure to enjoy part of your spare-time second-income fortune while you have it. Work is fun—but so is pleasure. Use your second income to give you and your family the things you've always wanted. Money is of little value until you put it to work doing good for yourself and others.

Money is worth little unless you get some pleasure from it every day of your life, and building a second-income spare-time fortune is not worth your time and effort unless the money gives you things you would not have otherwise. Though the first fourteen chapters of this book showed you the steps to follow in building your spare-time fortune, each hint aimed at the present chapter, which shows you how to be happy when wealthy. Let's see how you can build your life pattern around your second-income fortune. You'll learn that

15

Build Your
Life Pattern
Around Your Fortune

each spare-time dollar can be worth two dollars, or more, in happiness and contentment.

Never be ashamed of your wealth. Money is good, useful, constructive. Begin using your money from the first day your spare-time business shows a profit. Spend, as a start, some money on yourself—even if you spend only thirty-five cents for a hobby magazine. Reward yourself first, for you are the one who is doing the work. You are entitled to something extra, to a small reward that will be an incentive to greater effort on your part.

Next, reward your family—your wife, children, parents, and other relatives. You'll be most successful in building your second-income spare-time fortune if you have your wife's understanding and cooperation. So reward her with something she has wanted for years—a new coat, a rug for the living room, or some similar gift. Don't, unless she wants you to, buy her a Cadillac when this is what *you've* wanted for the last several years. Instead, buy a truly feminine gift, something she will enjoy because it's what she has wanted for a long while. Better yet, give her the money and allow her to choose her own gift. The shopping spree will delight her, as will the present she chooses.

Reward your children next. What boy of five or six doesn't want a special toy—a fire engine, model of a tugboat, or a tow truck? Remember, he's only five or six once in his life. You can give him the pleasure of an unusual toy or other present *now*. The joy he gets from the toy will bring back memories of your youth when you may have received a special gift, or it may recall the gifts you longed for but never received. The same is true also for your daughter. Seeing the pleasure your children get from your spare-time second income will give you greater drive, more enthusiasm, and clearer goals. Your income will rise along with the pleasures you obtain from it.

Do something for your parents with your second income. Though they may not need cash, a thoughtful present is always welcome. Most of us have fond memories of our parents, and their efforts to provide us with the right start in life. Doing something special for them now, while they are alive and able to enjoy our gift, is rewarding and gratifying to both our parents and ourselves. So do something now—today—while you have the money. You'll never regret a gift to your parents—or your wife's parents. But if you get into the habit of overlooking gifts, your parents may be gone from you before you can change your habits.

Once you've rewarded yourself, your wife, children, and parents, look at the other members of your family. Is there someone—a distant cousin, uncle, aunt—who needs help? Is anyone in the hospital or some other institution where a check or gift would be welcome? What about the children of your various relatives? Are any of the youngsters in school or college under circumstances where a check—even five dollars—would be welcome? Do a good turn today for one or more of these relatives and you'll be filled with a warm glow. What's more, your relatives will appreciate you more than you may think possible.

GET THE THINGS YOU WANT

After you've rewarded your loved ones, make plans for the things you'll buy in the future with the profits from your spare-time second income. Be sure to plan carefully because it is easy to make mistakes when spending money. Whenever I advise spare-time second-income fortune builders I recommend my "make-do" plan. This valuable plan releases the full power of your money, enabling you to get more from every dollar you spend. Here's how you can use this versatile plan in *your* life— beginning this very moment.

1. *Define, in general terms, exactly what you want.* Thus, you might list items like a newer car, a larger home, a bowling ball fitted to your hand, a pair of skis, a fund for your children's education.

2. *Decide how much you can afford to pay for each item.* Obtain at least three prices for each item. *Never* accept the first price given you. Instead, shop around; visit several dealers. Keep in mind at all times this important fact—*when you have money in your pocket you are king.* Before you agree to purchase any item you can bargain, haggle, insist on demonstrations, ask for and obtain proof of various claims, and obtain concessions that will make the purchase more attractive to you. *But once you buy an item you immediately lose your bargaining power.* So restrain yourself; never grab at the first offer made to you. Take every possible step to seek the best item at the lowest price.

3. *Analyze, before you buy, the worth of the service the product renders.* Thus, an auto provides transportation. Ask yourself, "What is this transportation worth to me?" Analyze the quality of the service a product renders by asking, "Is the transportation offered by a $6,000 car

worth $4,000 more, to me, than the transportation offered by one costing $2,000?" This approach allows you to apply one of the newest techniques —*value analysis*—to your personal and business life.

4. *Choose, wherever possible, the make-do solution to your problem.* Thus, in the case of the $6,000 vs the $2,000 auto, choose the lower-cost car because the transportation it offers is 99 per cent as good as the high-cost car. Sure, you'd look better in a $6,000 auto. It would give you prestige; your wife would be happier with it. But *unless an item contributes to the profits of your second-income spare-time fortune you should, in general, choose the lowest cost product offering acceptable service.* This make-do approach to your needs can save you thousands of dollars over a period of years. What's more, the savings you make on one item, such as a car, can be used to purchase another—like hobby equipment, home furnishings, or appliances.

Use this four-step make-do approach in every aspect of your life. Soon you'll find that your second-income spare-time fortune, coupled with the make-do approach to expenditures, is enabling you to live a full and enjoyable life. Thus, one spare-time fortune builder I know has two new autos (one a convertible), a twelve-room house, a thirty-foot boat, an excellent stock portfolio, a hefty savings account, and the newest and best of furnishings in his home—all because he uses a make-do approach toward his earnings. Both cars are compacts; his home is in a middle-class section of town; his boat is not the newest but it is in top-notch condition; he often buys as few as five shares of stock at a time. But as he said to me recently, "My possessions give me 99 per cent of the pleasure the millionaire gets from his. The make-do approach permits me to have everything I've ever wanted—a comfortable home, two cars, a boat, stocks, money in the bank." The make-do approach can do the same for you.

As you get the things you want, keep another important fact in mind: *don't tie too much money up in items that are difficult to sell* (houses, land, boats, airplanes, horses) *unless you intend to use and enjoy them.* If you want to speculate, buy and sell items that other people want, not what *you* want, unless your judgment is close to that of the buying public. Loading yourself with items that are difficult to sell when you don't make much use of them can lead to slow waste of your spare-time second-income fortune.

As the final step in acquiring the things you want, carry some of your profits in your wallet at all times. Select an amount that makes you feel good—$100, $200, $500. Having the money with you will enable you to buy the small things you want when you see them. More important is the safe, comfortable, secure feeling you'll have knowing there's a small "bundle" of money in your pocket. Those few thin bills in your wallet will spur you on, helping you build your life pattern around your spare-time second-income fortune.

USE YOUR WEALTH TO HELP OTHERS

Share your money with others—you will enjoy every dollar you spend to help others. Fred Annett, successful editor during the day, earned an excellent spare-time second income by writing books in the evening. Fred put some of his second income to good use by lending money to a young man to help pay for his college education. The young man repaid Fred after he graduated, but to this day he tells people how Fred's generous loan gave him the start in life he needed.

Contribute to your favorite charities—be they religious, educational, scientific, literary, medical, public service, or any other. You'll get a good feeling when you send your check in and the organization and its cause will benefit. You can contribute more than just money to charity, if you wish. Thus, if you have a summer camp, a boat, a backyard swimming pool, or similar facility, share it with some orphan children, underprivileged neighbors, and others who would enjoy it.

Helping others by contributing money or facilities is an excellent use of your wealth. Our nation is famous for the generous contributions made for public purposes. Think for a moment and you will quickly recognize the contributions made by the Rockefellers, Mellons, Carnegies, Kennedys, and many others. These men contributed to the public good because they wanted to help others. Doing so gave them great satisfaction. Victor Hugo recognized this when he said, "As the purse is emptied the heart is filled."

So don't put off helping others. Begin as soon as your spare-time business starts to show a profit. As Samuel Johnson wrote, "He who waits to do a great deal of good at once will never do anything." Using your wealth to help others will broaden your outlook on life and give you greater incentive to build a larger second-income fortune in your spare time. You benefit; the world benefits; someone is happier because you shared a small part of your wealth with others. All of us who earn a little more than the next man should strive to give until it hurts a little.

ENJOY THE BENEFITS OF YOUR FORTUNE

Don't become a tightwad—enjoy your fortune. Do what you enjoy —travel, play, loaf, help—now. If you don't enjoy your wealth now, I assure you your relatives will enjoy it after you are out of this life. Spend a little—save a little; but above all, *enjoy your money*.

Bring your family into the enjoyment of your fortune. Take trips together; buy the home and furnishings you and your wife dream of; send your children to good schools. Make your spare-time second-income profits part of their lives, as well as your own. Teach your youngsters the value of money, but make it possible for them to learn by giving them some money to manage. In my family I've allowed my children to select and buy a few shares of stock. Watching the changing value of their stock teaches them much about the American system and trains them to be alert to spare-time second-income possibilities in their own lives. You can do the same, or you can choose other ways to teach while sharing.

Everyone in the civilized world understands the purpose of money. Money is a universal language; pay a man for his efforts and he knows you are satisfied, regardless of what tongue he speaks. Money, wisely used, can bring you happiness, better health, greater joy, and more satisfaction in life. Combine these benefits with the fun, increase in knowledge, building of skills, and improved security you derive from a spare-time second-income fortune and you have an unbeatable combination.

This book shows you how and where to build your spare-time second-income fortune. Use its suggestions and you have an excellent chance of increasing your income. Begin today and watch your money grow. Meanwhile, from one spare-time, second-income fortune builder to another—good luck and enjoy your extra money!

Index

Fr. Jerome Romanowski
St. Gregory's